the great *mussel* and clam cookbook

whitecap

First published by: R&R Publications Marketing Pty. Ltd.
ACN 27 062 090 555
12 Edward Street, Brunswick Victoria 3056 Australia
©Richard Carroll

This edition published in 2004 in the U.S. and Canada by Whitecap Books Ltd.
For more information, contact:
Whitecap Books
351 Lynn Avenue
North Vancouver
British Columbia
Canada V7J 2C4

©Richard Carroll

Publisher: Richard Carroll
Production Manager: Anthony Carroll
Creative Director: Vincent Wee
Computer Manager: Paul Sims
Food Photography: Warren Webb
Food for Photography: Olivier Massart
Food Stylist: Di Kirby
Recipe Development: Ellen Argyriou and Olivier Massart, Tamara Milstein pages 10 and 70
Proof Reader: Fiona Brodribb
Editor of North American Edition: Marial Shea

The publishers would like to thank the management and staff of The Belgium Beer Café at 429 Miller St, Cammeray, Sydney for their assistance and skill in providing their product and food for presentation to photography.

The publishers would also like to thank Mr. John Mercer of the Marine & Freshwater Resources Institute, Queenscliffe, Victoria for the provision of photographs and information relating to mussel aquaculture used in this book.

National Library of Canada Cataloguing in Publication Data

Main entry under title:
The great mussel and clam cookbook / editor, Marial Shea ;
recipe developers, Ellen Argyriou, Olivier Massart and Tamara Milstein. -- North American ed.

(Great seafood series)
Includes index.

ISBN 1-55285-537-6
1. Cookery (Mussels) 2. Cookery (Clams) I. Argyriou, Ellen. II. Shea, Marial. III. Massart, Olivier. IV. Milstein, Tamara. V. Series.
TX753.G735 2003   641.6'94   C2003-911235-7

Computer Typeset in Verdana, Trojan and Charcoal

Printed in Indonesia

The publisher acknowledges the financial support of the Government of Canada through the Book Publishing Industry Development Program for our publishing activities.

contents

INTRODUCTION

Let us dive deep into the magical world of mussels and clams, closely related to oysters and scallops, but with a wonderful taste of their own.

Mussels and clams are part of a diverse group of mollusks which share the anatomical feature of a shell. While sometimes discarded in the creation of chowders, the shells have become an essential element in other recipes. They sustain the appearance of bite-sized morsels. To many chefs, the shell is just as important as the flesh in the presentation of a unique culinary experience.

In its natural state, the shell of the mussel or clam is sealed tight to guard against predators as well as the drying air during low tide. While the shells are commonly used in button making and the secreted pearls (usually of poorer quality than oysters) are found in inexpensive jewellery, it is the delicious visceral mass of the mollusks that has intrigued seafood lovers worldwide.

Most species of mussels and clams are edible, which makes them accessible to the masses rather than being the exclusive domain of the affluent. They are also available in the supermarket alongside other canned seafood, allowing even inlanders to enjoy the same tastes as their seaside counterparts. Mussels and clams are for all to enjoy.

Magnificent Mollusks!

Along with being widely available, mussels and clams are also versatile. Blended with exotic flavors, these magnificent mollusks can form the base of soups, salads, entrées or main dishes. A quick browse through this book will convince you of their versatility. Seasoned with the right combination of spices, mussels and clams can take on a brand new hue as well as an appetizing new taste.

This carefully selected collection of recipes is sure to cultivate a new appreciation for mussels and clams in even the most rigid diner. We have provided step-by-step instructions and beautiful illustrations to show you how easy it can be to impress your guests the next time you entertain. Remember that the presence of seafood on any table instantly lifts the standard of your meal. In particular, the neat, symmetrical shell and delectable taste embellish a dinner party with an upmarket ambience. Mussels and clams simply look good and taste great. They are an easy choice and a guaranteed winner.

If this pleasure to the palate isn't enough to convince the uncertain, then the fact that these shellfish have less fat that the average T-bone steak but are still full of nutrients might entice you. With so many reasons to make mussels and clams an addition to your list of food favorites, come out of your shell and discover a delectable delight from the deep blue.

MUSSELS

European mussels have been cultured since the thirteenth century. Currently, a number of species of mussels are farmed globally, the most common of which is the blue mussel.

China is now the largest producer of blue mussels in the world, its culture technique depending on a high proportion of spat being produced from hatcheries.

Other important producers of mussels are Spain, the Netherlands, Denmark and France.

Spat Collection

Mussel spat is generally collected from wild populations by spat collectors although artificial hatchery production is technically possible and increasingly prevalent.

Spat collectors are typically made of a fibrous, hairy-looking rope which is hung from longlines in areas which are known to have good mussel spat-fall. Spat collection ropes are hung in the water just in time for the peak spawning and spat-fall period. For commercial purposes, spat densities must be 1640ft/500m of collection rope or greater to be economical. A spat density of 3280ft/1000m of collection rope allows for sufficient growth without overcrowding.

High settlement densities of spat result in stunted growth and may result in excessive mortalities.

Juveniles are generally stripped from the ropes when they are 1/2in/12mm in length, for on-growing.

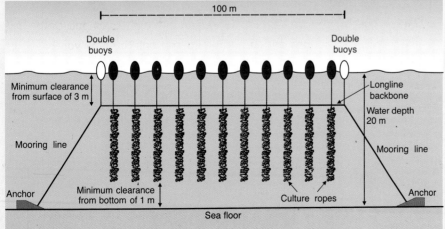

MUSSELS

Grow-Out

Once the juveniles have reached ½in/12mm in size on the spat collectors, they are ready to be re-seeded onto grow-out longlines. Re-seeding is a process whereby the juveniles are thinned out to encourage further growth of the mussels. This is a full-time job for

the farmers who, each day, weather permitting, take the collection ropes from the water to strip the mussels from the collection rope.

The juvenile mussels are separated from each other by passing them through a mussel de-clumping machine before they are fed through a funnel and onto a grow-out rope. A cotton stocking, also known as a mussock, is placed around the outside of the grow-out rope holding the juvenile mussels against the rope. As the mussels grow, they re-attach themselves

to the ropes by way of byssus threads. The mussock disintegrates, leaving the mussels. The mussels are then hung back in the water, and continue to grow for a further 8 to 12 months. The commercial stocking rate for mussels on grow-out lines is generally between 200 and 400 mussels per 3½ft/metre of rope. It is important to re-seed mussels when they are still juvenile spat because when mussels get larger than 1½in/40mm, they do not attach as readily to the rope. This means that slippage will occur with mussels slipping down and

MUSSELS

forming clumps in the bottom of the sock. This results in a reduced growth rate and poor shell shape. The stockings and rope are skewered and tied at 20in/0.5m intervals to ensure that the mussels are evenly distributed.

Ideally, grow-out farms are situated away from heavy spat settlement areas to avoid layers of spat attaching to larger mussels. Longlines require culling to remove naturally settling juvenile mussels.

Mortalities of mussels can occur if there is a lack of food in the area or if they are exposed to extreme wave action.

Growth

The growth rate of mussels on longlines will vary according to density, depth and food availability, with decreased growth experienced at high stocking densities and greater depths.

Growth rates of blue mussels vary but can be rapid. Blue mussels can reach 1¼–3½in/32–92mm in length after 12 months and 2–4½in/53–110mm after 18 months. Commercial harvest usually occurs after 1 to 2 years. As in other shellfish, the meat condition changes seasonally during the growing period. Male and female blue mussels mature within 2 years at 1½–2in/4.5–5cm in length, with mortality at its highest during the free-floating larval stage of the life cycle.

MUSSELS

Harvesting

Harvesting of blue mussels for market requires that the product be removed from the longlines and the shells cleaned of external fouling before presentation. This process is usually automated and involves a washer-tumbler machine in which the mussels are rotated and rubbed against each other to dislodge small mussels, barnacles and other fouling organisms. In some ideal growing areas where there are high levels of nutrients and phytoplankton, the mussels need to be transferred to more oceanic water to clean themselves before harvesting. There is a small window of opportunity for harvest each year. Harvest must be performed once the mussels are in their best meat condition but before they spawn. It is important that prospective mussel farmers determine when they can sell their stock as this will have considerable impact on their ability to supply markets. Some areas may have a very restricted harvest period and the condition of mussels will vary annually with some years being better than others. For this reason, it is important to keep records of conditions to determine site characteristics.

3.5oz/105g Cooked Meat	Common Mussel	T-Bone Steak
Calories	172	214
Protein	23.80 g	26.13 g
Fat	4.48 g	10.37 g
Carbohydrates	7.39 g	0.00 g
Cholesterol	56.00 g	80.00 g
Calcium	33.00 mg	7.00 mg
Magnesium	37.00 mg	26.00 mg
Phosphorus	285.00 mg	208.00mg
Potassium	268.00 mg	407.00 mg
Iron	6.72 mg	3.00 mg
Omega 3 Fatty Acids	782.00 mg	0.00 mg
Omega 6 Fatty Acids	36.00 mg	290.00 mg

Nutritional Value of Mussels (compared to T-Bone Steak)

CLAMS

Probably the first thing clams bring to mind is chowder. It's hard to beat a good bowl of clam chowder, whether you like it New England or Manhattan style. Maybe you prefer your clams au naturel, raw or steamed with little or no embellishment. Lucky you if you are in a location where you can dig your own, but clam-diggers need to familiarize themselves with the causes and consequences of paralytic shellfish poisoning before employing that clam rake. Clams can be as versatile as other shellfish if you dare to venture beyond the basics. Before we delve into the recipes, take a look at...

Clam History

The clam is a bi-valve mollusk of the *Pelecypoda* class that digs in the sand. Although native to both salt and fresh water, saltwater clams are considered far superior for eating. Clam comes from the Old English *clamm*, meaning "bond" or "fetter" relating to its tightly clamped shell. Native Americans carved clam shells into beads and used them as currency or *wampum* (Algonquian meaning "white string of beads"), and introduced colonists to the concept of clambakes. The National Marine Fisheries located in Milford, Connecticut, pioneered clam farming circa 1930. Commercial hatcheries gained a foothold in the Northeast in the 1960s. Most commercially available clams are raised on farms. Since the shells are built of calcium deposits, it's no wonder that clams are a good source of calcium and also high in protein.

Clam Varieties

Enjoyed as a food source since prehistoric times, there are over 2,000 varieties of clams. There are two main types of clam: hard-shell (*Mercenaria mercenaria*, from the Latin *merces* meaning "pay") and soft-shell (*Mya arenaria*). Hard-shell clams generally live in deeper waters, whereas soft-shell reside in tide flats. Soft-shells are generally not eaten raw. The siphon neck protrudes from soft-shells, so they cannot completely close their shell.

Clam Selection and Storage

Clams are found year-round in various forms, including fresh (both shucked and unshucked), frozen, and canned. They are best in cold-weather months, as they are susceptible to bacteria in summer months, but they are much easier to dig in summer. Whether shucked or unshucked, clams are highly perishable and should be eaten and/or cooked as soon as possible.

Shucked clams should be plump, smell fresh, and feel heavy for their size. Avoid those with an ammonia aroma. The clam juice should be clear with no shell fragments. Geoducks, if you can find them in the market, should have short, fat, unwrinkled necks. Wrinkling indicates they have been out of the water too long and are beginning to dehydrate. The flesh of clams can range from creamy white to gray to dark orange. Properly handled live clams will last two days in the refrigerator under optimum conditions.

CLAMS

Whole clams still in the shell must be sold live. Fresh, unshucked clams should be stored in a porous bag made of burlap or other natural material in the refrigerator. If you do not have cloth bags, store in a bowl covered with a wet cloth in the refrigerator, not on ice. Never store them in sealed plastic or submerged in water—they will die. Use preferably within 24 hours, although if they are truly fresh, they will last a few days under refrigeration. Discard any clams with shells that are open or that do not close when tapped, and any with broken shells. If you can jiggle the shell halves from side to side, it's a sure sign the clam is no longer living. For live soft-shell clams and geoducks, touch the siphon neck. If it moves, it's alive; if not, discard it. You can place the clams in a pot of water as another test, and discard any that float.

Do not freeze clams in their shells. To freeze clams, shuck them, being careful to save their liquid. Rinse with salt water (1 tablespoon of salt to 1 quart of water), and place in a container with the reserved clam liquid and additional salt water so they are completely covered. Frozen clams will last up to three months. Thaw frozen clams in the refrigerator before using, and never refreeze them. Cooked clams can be stored in a covered container in the refrigerator up to four days. Freezing is not recommended for cooked clams as they will become extremely tough and rubbery.

Fresh Clam Preparation

First, scrub the outside of the clams thoroughly with a stiff brush. Since clams naturally burrow in the sand, they need to be purged of grit lest crunching down on grains of sand diminish your enjoyment of this flavorful seafood. Sand should be removed before cooking by covering the clams with salt and letting sit for several hours. Adding 1/4 to 1/2 cup of cornmeal to the soaking water helps expel the dark matter and sand from the stomachs and also whitens the meat.

If you are shucking your own, the shells will be easier to open if you freeze them for 15 to 20 minutes.

Remove from freezer and let sit a few minutes before attacking the shells. As they warm up, the muscles relax and the shells will open slightly so you can get your clam knife in. Remember to shuck over a bowl to save all that wonderful juice known as clam liquor.

You may wish to remove the tough skin covering the neck of longneck clams. Slit the skin lengthwise and remove it. You can grind the skin and add it to chowder or creamed clam dishes.

Clam Usage

If clams do not open after cooking, discard them as it means they were not alive and may be contaminated with bacteria or toxins. Clams can be substituted for most oyster, scallop, and mussel recipes and vice versa. The smallest clams are the most desirable for eating raw. The larger they get, the tougher the meat. Extended heat further toughens the meat, so cook gently at low heat settings.

SOUPS & SALADS

San Franciscan Seafood Chowder

INGREDIENTS

8 small round loaves of bread
1/4 cup/50mL butter
2 leeks, finely sliced
2 onions, finely chopped
4 cloves garlic, minced
2 carrots, peeled and chopped
1 parsnip, peeled and chopped
2 stalks celery, finely sliced
1 tablespoon/15mL fresh thyme leaves
1/2 cup/125mL all-purpose flour
8 cups/2L fish stock
2lb/1kg mixed seafood, including
   prawns (shrimp), mussels, clams,
   calamari (squid), white fish
1 cup/250mL whipping or Devon cream
1 cup/250mL fresh parsley, chopped
salt and pepper, to taste
juice of 1 large lemon
1/2 bunch chives, chopped, for garnish

METHOD

1. Preheat the oven to 400°F/200°C. First, prepare bread for bowls. Using a sharp knife, cut a large hole in the top of the bread loaf, then remove this crusty top and set aside. Carefully remove all the soft bread from the inside of the loaf (leaving the surrounding crust intact).

2. Place the loaves in the preheated oven and bake for 15 minutes (until the loaves are crisp and dry). Set aside.

3. Melt the butter in a large saucepan and add the leeks, onions, garlic, carrots, parsnip, celery and thyme leaves. Sauté for 10 minutes until the vegetables are soft and golden. Remove the pan from the heat and sprinkle the flour over the vegetables, stirring constantly to mix the flour with the butter. Return the pan to the heat and continue stirring until the mixture begins to turn golden (about 2 minutes). This gives the flour a cooked flavor.

4. Add the fish stock stirring constantly to dissolve the roux mixture into the liquid, then simmer the soup for 20 minutes. Meanwhile, prepare the seafood by cutting the fish and shellfish into bite-sized pieces.

5. Add all the seafood, cream, parsley and salt and pepper, and cook for a further 5 minutes. (Do not allow the soup to boil rapidly because it may curdle.) Once the seafood has cooked, stir the lemon juice through the fish and ladle the soup into the bread bowls. Garnish with some chopped chives and serve.

Serves 8

SAN FRANSISCAN SEAFOOD CHOWDER

Hot and Sour Soup

INGREDIENTS

4 red or golden shallots, sliced
2 fresh green chilies, chopped
6 kaffir lime leaves
4 slices fresh ginger
8 cups/2L fish, chicken or vegetable stock
8oz/250g boneless firm fish fillets,
    cut into chunks
12 medium uncooked prawns (shrimp),
    shelled and deveined
12 mussels, scrubbed and beards removed
1½ cups/375mL oyster or straw
    mushrooms
3 tablespoons/45mL lime juice
2 tablespoons/25mL Thai fish sauce
    (nam pla)
chopped cilantro and lime wedges

METHOD

1. Place the shallots, chilies, lime leaves, ginger and stock in a saucepan and bring to the boil over a high heat. Reduce the heat and simmer for 3 minutes.

2. Add the fish, prawns (shrimp), mussels and mushrooms and cook for 3–5 minutes or until the fish and seafood are cooked. Discard any mussels that do not open after 5 minutes of cooking. Stir in the lime juice and fish sauce. To serve, ladle the soup into bowls, scatter with cilantro and accompany with lime wedges.

Serves 6

Clam Chowder

INGREDIENTS

1 cup/250mL butter
6 strips of bacon, finely chopped
3 onions, finely chopped
1½ cups/375mL finely
    chopped celery
1 cup/250mL all-purpose flour
4 cups/1L milk
3 cups/750mL fish stock
1lb/500g potatoes, finely diced
    (3 medium)
2lb/1kg clam meat
salt and pepper
cream and chopped fresh parsley
    for serving

METHOD

1. Heat the butter in a saucepan and cook the bacon, onion and celery until tender.

2. Add the flour and cook for 2 minutes.

3. Add the milk, fish stock and potatoes, cover and simmer for 10 minutes.

4. Add the clam meat and cook again for 10 minutes. Season to taste.

5. Serve in a deep plate with cream and parsley.

Serves 6-8

HOT AND SOUR SOUP

CLAM CHOWDER

Mussel Soup

INGREDIENTS

1¼ cups/300mL water

1 small carrot, finely diced

½ cup/125mL cauliflower, florets

½ red bell pepper, finely diced

½ onion, finely diced

pinch saffron

10 coriander seeds, cracked

3 tablespoons/45mL sherry vinegar

¼ cup/50mL butter

2 tablespoons/25mL all-purpose flour

2lb/1kg mussels, cooked mariniéres
  style, reserving cooking broth
  (see page 48)

2 tablespoons/25mL heavy or
  whipping cream

1 tablespoon/15mL parsley, finely chopped

METHOD

1. Place the water, carrot, cauliflower, red bell pepper, onion, saffron and coriander seeds in a large pot over high heat. Bring to the boil and add the vinegar.

2. Remove from the heat and allow to cool down. When cold, strain the vegetables from the cooking liquid.

3. In a cooking pot over medium heat, melt the butter then add the flour. Stir with a wooden spoon and cook gently for 2 minutes.

4. Add the broth slowly with a whisk and cook until slightly thickened and smooth in consistency.

5. Add the reserved vegetables, mussels and cream and bring to the boil. Add salt and pepper to taste. Garnish with parsley just before serving.

Serves 4

Clam Bisque

INGREDIENTS

1lb/500g white fish fillets

3 cups/750mL milk

salt and pepper, to taste

⅛ teaspoon/1mL nutmeg

1 bay leaf

8oz/250g jar mussels

2 tablespoons/25mL butter

1 medium-sized onion, finely chopped

2 stalks celery, finely cubed

3 tablespoons/45mL all-purpose flour

1 tablespoon/15mL lemon juice

1 tablespoon/15mL finely chopped
  parsley or chives

1–2 tablespoons/15-25mL dry sherry

¼ cup/50mL cream

METHOD

1. Cut the fish fillets into ¾in/2cm squares. Place in a saucepan with the milk, salt, pepper, nutmeg and bay leaf. Bring gently to the boil, then simmer slowly for 10 minutes. Stand covered for 10 minutes to infuse the flavors. Strain the milk from the fish and reserve. Keep the fish warm.

2. Drain the liquid from the mussels and rinse in cold water. Cut the mussels into 2 or 3 pieces.

3. Melt the butter in a large saucepan, add the onion and celery and cook gently for 10 minutes without browning. When soft, stir in the flour and cook for 1 minute while stirring.

4. Remove the saucepan from the heat and gradually stir in the reserved milk, stirring well after each addition until free from lumps. Return to the heat and stir until the mixture boils and thickens.

5. Add the lemon juice, chopped mussels, chopped parsley or chives, sherry and cooked fish. Simmer slowly for 10 minutes. Stir in the cream and simmer for 5 minutes more. Serve in individual bowls, with croutons if desired.

Serves 4–6

MUSSEL SOUP

Clam and Black Mussel Broth

INGREDIENTS

3 tablespoons/45mL vegetable oil
1 onion finely chopped
2 tablespoons/25mL Tom Yum
  (spicy Thai) paste
8oz/250g clams, cleaned and free of sand
8oz/250g black mussels, cleaned
1 cup/250mL chicken stock
1 stalk lemon grass, chopped
juice of 1 lime
1 tablespoon cilantro stalk and roots,
  finely chopped
1 tablespoon/15mL Thai fish sauce
1 tablespoon/15mL fresh cilantro,
  roughly chopped

Method

1. Heat the oil in a wok or large cooking pot. Add the onion, Tom Yum, clams and mussels. Simmer, covered with a lid, for 30 seconds.

2. Add the chicken stock, lemon grass, lime juice, cilantro stalk and roots, Thai fish sauce and stir through. Cook until all shells have opened.

3. Add the fresh cilantro and serve in soup bowls.

Serves 6

CLAM AND BLACK MUSSEL BROTH

MUSSEL, BELGIAN ENDIVE AND BASIL SOUP

Mussel, Belgian Endive and Basil Soup

INGREDIENTS

2lb/1kg black mussels, cooked
  mariniéres style and removed
  from shell (see page 48)
2 tablespoons/25mL butter
2 Belgian endives, leaves cut
1 cup/250mL broth from cooking the
  mussels, strained
2 tablespoons/25mL whipping cream
  or thickened cream
15 basil leaves, chopped finely
salt and pepper, to taste

METHOD

1. Prepare mussels, reserving broth.

2. Melt the butter in a pot and stir-fry the Belgian endive.

3. Add the broth, cream and basil. Mix well and whip until the ingredients are all blended. Season with salt and pepper.

4. Add the mussels, heat until boiling and serve in bowls.

Serves 4

Maltese Mussels

INGREDIENTS

1/2 cup/125mL olive oil
1 onion, diced
3 garlic cloves, chopped
2 roasted bell peppers,
    peeled and diced
1/2 bulb fennel, diced
1/2 celery stalk, diced
2/3 cup/150mL white wine
1 orange, juice plus grated zest
1 cup/250mL tomato juice
2 cups/500mL chicken stock
salt and pepper
cayenne pepper and paprika
1lb/500g black mussels, cleaned

METHOD

1. In a large pot on medium heat, add the oil, onion, garlic, bell peppers, fennel and celery. Cook for 10 minutes.

2. Add the white wine, orange juice, zest, tomato juice, chicken stock, seasoning and cook for 20 minutes.

3. Add the mussels and cook until all the mussels have opened, about 8–10 minutes.

4. Serve with wood-fired bread or grissini (Italian breadsticks).

Serves 6

Manhattan Chowder

INGREDIENTS

5lb/2.2kg mussels
4 strips bacon, rind removed, diced
1 large onion, chopped
1 bay leaf
1 green bell pepper, finely diced
2 stalks celery, diced
1lb/500g peeled and diced potatoes
    (3 medium)
2 x 14oz/398mL cans peeled tomatoes,
    seeds removed, chopped
salt and pepper to taste

METHOD

1. Wash and scrub the mussels and steam them open. Remove and discard the shells, reserving the mussels. Strain the cooking liquor through fine muslin and add enough water to measure 4 cups/1L.

2. In a heavy pan, cook the bacon gently until it begins to crisp. Add the onion and the bay leaf and sauté until the onion is tender, about 8 minutes. Add the bell pepper and celery and sauté for a further few minutes.

3. Add the potatoes and tomatoes with the juice, the mussel cooking liquid, and salt and pepper to taste. Bring to the boil and simmer, covered, for 20 minutes, until the potatoes are tender. Discard the bay leaf, add the mussels and cook a further 5–10 minutes. Season the chowder with a little Tabasco.

Serves 4–6

MALTESE MUSSELS

Cold Marinated Mussel Salad

INGREDIENTS

1 small carrot, diced finely

1/2 cup/125mL cauliflower, broken
   into florets

1/2 red bell pepper, diced finely

1/2 onion, diced finely

pinch saffron

10 coriander seeds, cracked

3 tablespoons/45mL sherry vinegar

10oz/285g cooked mussel meat
   [equivalent to approximately 2lb/1kg
   mussels in their shells, cooked
   mariniéres style and chilled
   (see page 48)]

1¹/₄ cups/285mL water

Salad:

handful mesclun salad mix

cherry tomatoes, quartered

3 tablespoons/45mL virgin olive oil

salt and pepper

METHOD

1. Place the carrot, cauliflower, bell pepper, onion, saffron and coriander seeds in water to cover in a pot over high heat.

2. Bring to the boil and add the vinegar.

3. Remove from the heat straight away and allow to cool down. When cold, strain the vegetables and discard the cooking liquid.

4. In a large salad bowl, mix together the mesclun, tomatoes, olive oil, vegetables and mussels. Season with salt and pepper.

Serves 4–6

Scandinavian Mussels

INGREDIENTS

$^1/2$ cup/125mL water

$^1/2$ onion, finely chopped

$^1/2$ stalk celery, finely chopped

$^1/2$ red bell pepper, finely chopped

1 tablespoon/15mL sugar

2 tablespoons/25mL white vinegar

2lb/1kg black mussels cleaned, cooked
  mariniéres style and removed
  from the shell (see page 48)

4 tablespoons/60mL mayonnaise

1 tablespoon/15mL chopped parsley

juice of 1 lemon

salt and pepper to taste

green salad or potato salad to serve

METHOD

1. In a small cooking pot, bring water, onion, celery, bell pepper, sugar and vinegar to the boil for 1 minute and set aside to cool.

2. Remove vegetables from liquid.

3. Mix mussels, mayonnaise, vegetables, parsley and lemon juice in a bowl, add salt and pepper.

4. Serve cold with green salad or a cold potato salad.

Serves 2

Seafood Paella Salad

INGREDIENTS

4 cups/1L chicken stock
1lb/500g uncooked large prawns
 (shrimp)
1 uncooked lobster tail (optional)
1lb/500g mussels in shells, cleaned
2 tablespoons/25mL olive oil
1 onion, chopped
2 ham steaks, cut into $1/2$ in/1cm cubes
2 cups/500mL arborio rice
$1/2$ teaspoon/2mL ground turmeric
$3/4$ cup/175mL fresh or frozen peas
1 red bell pepper, diced

Garlic Dressing
$1/2$ cup/125mL olive oil
$1/4$ cup/50mL white wine vinegar
3 tablespoons/45mL mayonnaise
2 cloves garlic, crushed
2 tablespoons/25mL chopped
 fresh parsley
freshly ground black pepper

METHOD

1. Place the stock in a large saucepan and bring to the boil. Add the prawns (shrimp) and cook for 1–2 minutes or until the prawns change color. Remove and set aside. Add the lobster tail and cook for 5 minutes or until the lobster changes color and is cooked. Remove and set aside. Add the mussels and cook until the shells open – discard any mussels that do not open after 5 minutes. Remove and set aside. Strain the stock and reserve. Peel and devein the prawns (shrimp), leaving the tails intact. Refrigerate the seafood until just prior to serving.

2. Heat the oil in a large saucepan, add the onion and cook for 4–5 minutes or until soft. Add the ham, rice and turmeric and cook, stirring, for 2 minutes. Add the reserved stock and bring to the boil. Reduce the heat, cover and simmer for 15 minutes or until the liquid is absorbed and the rice is cooked and dry. Stir in the peas and red bell pepper and set aside to cool. Cover and refrigerate for at least 2 hours.

3. To make the dressing, place the oil, vinegar, mayonnaise, garlic, parsley and black pepper to taste in a food processor or blender and process to combine.

4. To serve, place the seafood and rice in a large salad bowl, spoon over the dressing and toss to combine.

Serves 6

Mussel and Rice Salad

INGREDIENTS

3 cups/750mL chicken stock
$1^1/2$ cups/375mL long-grain rice
$4^1/2$lb/2kg mussels, scrubbed
$3/4$ cup/180mL white wine
2 teaspoons/10mL chopped tarragon
 or 1 teaspoon/5mL dried
water for mussels

Dressing
1 tablespoon/15mL wine vinegar
2 teaspoons/10mL Dijon mustard
salt and freshly ground pepper
4 tablespoons/60mL olive oil
2 tablespoons/25mL chopped parsley

METHOD

1. Bring the stock to the boil and add in the rice. Bring to the boil again, cover and cook gently until the rice is tender and the stock absorbed, about 18 minutes. Steam the mussels in the wine, tarragon and a little water. Remove the mussels from their shells leaving a few in the half shell for garnishing, if desired. Reserve half the cooking liquid.

2. Add the mussels to the rice. Strain reserved cooking liquid into a pan. Reduce over a high heat and sprinkle over the rice and mussels.

3. Mix the vinegar and mustard together with salt and pepper. Whisk in the oil, a little at a time, to make a thick dressing. Add to the salad and toss lightly. Cool to room temperature and toss gently with the parsley. Arrange on 6 to 8 serving plates with salad greens.

Serves 6–8

SEAFOOD PAELLA SALAD

Belgian Endive Salad with Clams and Mussels

INGREDIENTS

Marinated Vegetables

1 carrot, peeled and sliced

1/2 onion, sliced in half

1/2 stalk celery

15 coriander seeds, cracked

salt and pepper

2 tablespoons/25mL sherry vinegar

1 cup/250mL water

14oz/400g clams cooked and
   out of the shells

14oz/400g mussels cooked
   and out of the shells

2 Belgian endives, cut with leaves loose

4 slices of prosciutto, cooked under
   the grill and broken into small pieces

3 tablespoons/45mL virgin olive oil

1 tablespoon/15mL lemon juice

salt and pepper, to taste

METHOD

1. To prepare the marinated vegetables, place the ingredients together in a pot and boil for 2 minutes. Set aside to cool. When cold remove the liquid and keep the vegetables aside.

2. Mix all the other ingredients together with the marinated vegetables.

3. Refridgerate for 15 minutes until chilled.

4. Serve with crispy bread or Italian grissini (breadsticks).

Serves 6–8

Mussels and Prawns in Avocado Vinaigrette

INGREDIENTS

1 dozen medium mussels, cooked
   mariniéres stlye, reserving some of
   the broth (see page 48)

8 large green prawns (shrimp),
   shells removed

Dressing

1 avocado

2 1/2 tablespoons/35mL fresh lemon juice

4 tablespoons/60mL olive oil

salt and freshly ground pepper

1/4 teaspoon/1mL Dijon mustard

1 teaspoon/5mL grated onion

1/4 teaspoon/1mL paprika

shredded lettuce

minced parsley

METHOD

1. Shell the mussels and place them in a bowl with a little of the liquid in which they have cooked to keep them moist. Cook the prawns in the remaining mussel liquid for 1–2 minutes. Cool and shell.

2. To prepare the dressing, peel the avocado and remove the pit. Cut the avocado in pieces and place in a processor with the lemon juice. Blend until smooth. Gradually add the olive oil. Season very well with salt and pepper and add the mustard, onion and paprika. (May be prepared ahead.)

3. Arrange the mussels and prawns attractively on a bed of shredded lettuce. Cover with the avocado dressing and sprinkle with parsley. Serve cold or at room temperature.

Serves 2

BELGIAN ENDIVE SALAD WITH CLAMS AND MUSSELS

Mixed Shellfish and Potato Salad

INGREDIENTS

Dressing
5 tablespoons/75mL olive oil

1 tablespoons/15mL cider vinegar

1 teaspoon/5mL English mustard

salt and pepper, to taste

1¹/2lb/750g waxy potatoes, unpeeled

4 small cooked beets, diced

1 head fennel, finely sliced,
   plus feathery top, chopped

2lb/1kg mussels

1lb/500g clams

1¹/4 cups/300mL dry white wine
   or cider

1 shallot, finely chopped

4 green onions, finely sliced

3 tablespoons/45mL chopped
   fresh parsley

METHOD

1. To make the dressing, whisk together the oil, vinegar, mustard and seasoning. Boil the potatoes in salted water for 15 minutes or until tender, then drain. Cool for 30 minutes, then peel and slice. Place in a bowl and toss with half the dressing. Toss the beets and fennel with the rest of the dressing.

2. Scrub the mussels and clams under cold running water, pulling away any beards from the mussels. Discard any shellfish that are open or damaged. Place the wine or cider and shallot in a large saucepan and bring to the boil. Simmer for 2 minutes, then add the shellfish. Cover and cook briskly for 3–5 minutes, shaking the pan often, or until the shellfish have opened. Discard any that remain closed. Reserve the pan juices, set aside a few mussels in their shells and shell the rest.

3. Boil the pan juices for 5 minutes or until reduced to 1–2 tablespoons/15–25mL. Strain over the potatoes. Add the shellfish, green onions and parsley, then toss. Serve with the beet and fennel salad and garnish with the fennel tops and mussels in their shells.

Serves 4

LIGHT MEALS

Smoked Mussel Fritters

INGREDIENTS

2 x 3¹/₂oz/85g cans smoked mussels,
  drained
¹/₂ cup/125g all-purpose flour
1 teaspoon/5mL baking powder
1 teaspoon/5mL salt
1 small red bell pepper,
  seeded and finely diced
2 tablespoons/25mL chopped fresh cilantro
¹/₂ teaspoon/2mL cayenne pepper
1 egg, lightly beaten
¹/₄ cup/50mL beer
1 tablespoon/15mL lime juice
vegetable oil, for deep frying

Sauce
4 tablespoons/60mL mayonnaise
1 teaspoon/5mL wholegrain mustard
juice ¹/₂ lime
¹/₂ teaspoon/2mL clear honey

lime wedges, to serve

METHOD

1. Roughly chop the mussels and place in a bowl with the flour, baking powder, salt, red bell pepper, cilantro and cayenne and stir well.

2. Beat in the egg, beer and lime juice to form a soft dropping batter.

4. Heat the oil in a wok or deep frying pan over high heat. Drop tablespoonfuls of the mussel batter, in batches, into the hot oil. Fry for 3 minutes until golden. Drain on paper towels and keep warm in a moderate oven while cooking the rest.

5. Mix all the sauce ingredients together in a bowl. Serve the fritters with the sauce and some lime wedges to squeeze over.

Serves 4–6

Clam Provençal

INGREDIENTS

¹/₂ cup/125mL virgin olive oil
1 onion, finely chopped
1 red bell pepper, diced
4 vine-ripened tomatoes, diced
¹/₂ stalk celery, sliced
2 cloves garlic
2lb/1kg clams, cleaned and sand removed
²/₃ cup/150mL dry white wine
1 tablespoon/15mL freshly chopped
  aromatic herbs (thyme, rosemary,
  marjoram)
salt and pepper

METHOD

1. Place the oil, onion, bell pepper, tomatoes, celery and garlic in a large cooking pot. Cook over high heat for 5 minutes, stirring frequently to prevent sticking.

2. Add the clams, white wine, fresh herbs and seasoning and cook with the lid on until all the shells have opened. Stir frequently to ensure even cooking.

3. When the clams are open, serve large bowls with salad or grilled, sliced baguette. Complement the dis with a rosé or white wine from Provence.

Serves 4–6

CLAM PROVENÇAL

Baked Mussels

INGREDIENTS

30 medium mussels
2 shallots, finely chopped
1 sprig thyme
2 sprigs parsley
1 bay leaf
1/2 teaspoon/2mL salt
1/2 cup/125mL white wine
1/2 cup/125mL butter or
   margarine, softened
1 tablespoon/15mL parsley, chopped
2 cloves garlic, crushed
1 tablespoon/15mL chives

METHOD

1. Scrape the beard, and wash the mussels thoroughly and place in a large saucepan with the shallots, thyme, parsley and bay leaf.

2. Sprinkle the salt over and then add the wine. Steam for 5 minutes or until the shells have opened. Open the mussels and discard the lids.

3. Divide the mussels in the remaining half shells into 4 ovenproof dishes. Make a herb butter by combining the butter, parsley, garlic and chives and place a generous portion on each mussel.

4. Bake at 375°F/190°C for approximately 3 minutes or until the butter has melted.

Serves 4

Grilled Mussels

INGREDIENTS

20 large fresh mussels
1 cup/250mL basil leaves
1 clove garlic, crushed
1 small red chili, de-seeded and diced
1/2 teaspoon/2mL grated lemon rind
1 tablespoon/15mL pine nuts
1 tablespoon/15mL grated Parmesan
   cheese
1 tablespoon/15mL fresh breadcrumbs
salt and pepper
3–4 tablespoons/45–60mL extra virgin
   olive oil

METHOD

1. Wash and scrub the mussels. Steam the mussels with just the water on their shells, for 4 minutes until they have just opened. Discard any which do not open. Immediately plunge the mussels into cold water and drain again.

2. Remove the mussels from the pan and carefully discard one half of each shell. Arrange the remaining mussels in 1 large dish or 4 individual gratin dishes.

3. In a blender or food processor combine the basil, garlic, chili, lemon rind, pine nuts, Parmesan and half of the breadcrumbs. Pulse briefly to form a smooth paste and season to taste with salt and pepper.

4. Transfer the basil paste to a bowl and stir in the oil. Spoon a little of the paste over each mussel and finally top each one with a few more breadcrumbs. Cook under a preheated grill for 2–3 minutes until bubbling and golden. Serve at once.

Serves 4

BAKED MUSSELS

Black Forest Mussels with Mushrooms and Brandy

INGREDIENTS

2 tablespoons/25mL butter

1/2 onion, finely chopped

1³/4 cups/425mL finely sliced Black
   Forest mushrooms or field mushrooms

1 clove garlic, chopped

2lb/1kg black mussels, cleaned

1/2 cup/125mL white wine

salt and pepper to taste

2 tablespoons/25mL whipping or
   Devon cream

2 tablespoons/25mL brandy

parsley (optional)

METHOD

1. Place the butter, onions, mushrooms and garlic in a pot and cook over high heat for 5 minutes.

2. Add the mussels, white wine and seasoning.

3. Cook the mussels until all mussels have opened, stirring frequently.

4. Add the cream and stir for 30 seconds. Add the brandy and cook for another 1 minute.

5. Serve garnished with fresh parsley if desired.

Serves 4

Fried Vongole

INGREDIENTS

2 eggs, lightly beaten

salt and pepper

2 cups/500mL breadcrumbs

1 tablespoon/15mL dry mixed aromatic herbs

2lb/1kg clams, cleaned, cooked mariniéres
**   style and removed from shell (see page 48)**

oil for deep frying

3 tablespoons/45mL tartar sauce

METHOD

1. Place the eggs in a bowl and season with a little salt and pepper.

2. Combine the breadcrumbs and herbs in a separate bowl.

3. Dip the clams in the egg mixture, then roll in breadcrumbs.

4. Deep-fry the clams in hot oil, until golden brown.

5. Drain on paper towels and serve immediately with tartar sauce.

Serves 4

FRIED VONGOLE

Clams with White Wine and Garlic

INGREDIENTS
1¹/₂ lb/750g medium to small clams

salt

3 tablespoons/45mL olive oil

1 small onion, peeled and finely chopped

3 cloves garlic, peeled and minced

1 tablespoon/15mL all-purpose flour

¹/₂ cup/125mL dry white wine

pinch of paprika

1 bay leaf

salt and pepper

METHOD
1. Wash the clams well. Leave them in cold, lightly salted water for about an hour to get rid of any grit they may have in them.

2. Heat the oil in a frying pan. Add the onion and garlic and sauté until golden brown. Add the clams and cook over medium heat until the shells open. Add the flour and stir in well. Pour in the wine, add the paprika, bay leaf and some salt and pepper to taste. Continue cooking for a further 5 minutes.

3. Remove the bay leaf and serve the clams in the sauce. Half the fun is to eat the clam and then spoon up some sauce using the shell as a spoon.

Serves 4

Mussels with Tomatoes and Wine

INGREDIENTS

Tomato and Smoked Salmon Sauce

2 teaspoons/10mL olive oil

2 cloves garlic, crushed

2 shallots, chopped

2–3 slices smoked salmon,
  sliced into thin strips

1 red bell pepper, sliced

1 tablespoon/15mL no-added-salt
  tomato paste

14oz/398mL canned no-added-salt
  diced tomatoes

2 tablespoons/25mL chopped fresh parsley

2lb/1kg fresh mussels, scrubbed and
  beards removed

1 shallot, chopped

1 cup/250mL dry white wine

chopped fresh chives

METHOD

1. For the sauce, heat the oil in a non-stick frying pan over a medium heat. Add the garlic and shallots. Cook, stirring, for 1–2 minutes. Add the salmon and red bell pepper. Cook, stirring, for 3 minutes. Stir in the tomato paste. Cook for 3–4 minutes or until it becomes deep red and develops a rich aroma. Add the tomatoes. Cook, stirring, for 5 minutes or until the mixture starts to thicken. Stir in the parsley. Keep warm.

2. Meanwhile, place the mussels, shallot and wine in a large saucepan over a high heat. Cover. Bring to the boil then reduce the heat. Cook for 5 minutes or until the mussels open. Discard any mussels that do not open after 5 minutes of cooking.

3. Add the sauce to the mussels. Toss to combine.

4. To serve, divide the mixture among deep bowls. Scatter with chives. Accompany with crusty bread and a glass of red wine.

Serves 4

Seafood Escabeche

INGREDIENTS

16 large mussels, scrubbed

8oz/250g baby calamari (squid), cleaned

8oz/250g peeled small prawns (shrimp),
  deveined

2 cloves garlic, chopped

1 small red chili, de-seeded and chopped

1/4 cup/50mL dry sherry

1 tablespoon/15mL chopped basil,
  to garnish

bread, to serve

Marinade

2/3 cup/150mL extra virgin olive oil

2 shallots, chopped

3 tablespoons/45mL white wine vinegar

pinch sugar

1 tablespoon/15mL drained and chopped
  capers in brine

salt and pepper

METHOD

1. Prepare the seafood. Remove any beard still attached to the mussels. Cut the squid into rings and the tentacles in half, if large, and wash well. Wash and dry the raw prawns (shrimp).

2. Place the mussels into a pan with the garlic, chili and sherry. Cover and steam for 4–5 minutes until all the mussels are opened (discard any that remain closed). Remove the mussels with a slotted spoon and set aside.

3. Poach the prawns (shrimp) in the mussel liquid for 4–5 minutes until cooked. Poach the calamari (squid) for 2–3 minutes until cooked. Remove with a slotted spoon and add to the mussels. Reserve 2 tablespoons/25mL of the cooking liquid and leave to cool.

4. Combine all the marinade ingredients and stir in the reserved poaching liquid. Pour over the cold seafood, toss well and chill for several hours.

5. Return the escabeche to room temperature for 1 hour, scatter over the basil and serve with bread.

Serves 4

MUSSELS WITH
TOMATOES AND
WINE

Seafood Stew

INGREDIENTS

1/4 cup/50mL olive oil

12 mussels in their shells, scrubbed

2 onions, thinly sliced in rings

salt and pepper

3 tomatoes, sliced thickly

2lb/1kg white fish fillets

8oz/250g calamari (squid),
   cut into strips or rings

1 green bell pepper, sliced in rings

1 cup/250mL dry white wine

3 tablespoons/45mL chopped parsley

METHOD

1. Pour a little of the oil into a large heavy-based saucepan and arrange the scrubbed mussels over the base. Cover with a layer of onion rings and sprinkle with a little salt and pepper.

2. Place the tomato slices over the onions and season. Drizzle a little oil over the tomatoes. Place the fish and calamari (squid) in layers over the tomato. Season each layer and drizzle with a little oil.

3. Place a layer of green bell pepper rings on top. Pour in the white wine.

4. Cover and cook over a slow heat for 20–25 minutes until the fish flakes.

5. Spoon into individual soup bowls and sprinkle with chopped parsley. Serve with crusty bread.

Serves 6–8

Spaghettini with Baby Clams, Chili and Garlic

INGREDIENTS

14oz/400g spaghettini

1/4 cup/50mL olive oil

4 cloves garlic, sliced

4 red chilies, finely chopped

2 cups/500mL tomatoes, finely diced

680mL/24oz canned baby clams,
   or fresh, if available

1/3 cup/75mL parsley, chopped

juice of 2 lemons

salt and freshly ground black pepper

METHOD

1. Cook the spaghettini in boiling water with a little oil until al dente. Run under cold water until cold and set aside.

2. Heat half the oil and cook the garlic on a low heat until beginning to change color. Add the chilies and tomatoes, and cook for a few minutes.

3. Add the clams, parsley, lemon juice, remaining oil, spaghettini and a little of the water used to cook the clams, and heat through for a further 5 minutes. Season with salt and black ground pepper to taste.

Serves 4-6

Note: If using fresh clams, wash under running water, scraping the shells with a sharp knife or scourer. Place them in a large pan with a little water over a gentle heat until they open. Discard any that do not open.

LEEK AND SEEDED MUSTARD MUSSELS

Leek and Seeded Mustard Mussels

INGREDIENTS

2 tablespoons/25mL butter

1 leek sliced finely (do not use all the
green leaves; cut halfway as they get
bitter at the end of the plant.)

2lb/1kg black mussels, cleaned

3 tablespoons/45mL seeded mustard

1/2cup/125mL dry white wine

2 tablespoons/25mL Devon or
whipping cream

1 tablespoon/15mL chopped parsley

salt and pepper

METHOD

1. Place butter in a pot over high heat. Add leeks and cook for 1 minute.

2. Add mussels, seeded mustard and white wine.

3. Cook mussels until all have opened, stirring frequently for even cooking.

4. Add cream and parsley, stir for 15 seconds on high heat. Season with salt and pepper to taste.

Serves 4

Clams with Vinegar

INGREDIENTS

285mL/10oz can baby clams, drained
and well chilled

1 tablespoon/15mL white wine vinegar

METHOD

1. Simply mix the clams with the vinegar and serve cold as part of an antipasto plate.

Serves 4

Mussel and Zucchini Gratin

INGREDIENTS

$4^1/_2$lb/2kg mussels
small bunch finely chopped shallots
bay leaf
$^2/_3$ cup/150mL dry white wine
1kg/$2^1/_4$ lb zucchini (2 large or 3 small)
salt and freshly ground pepper
$^1/_4$ cup/50mL olive oil
$1^1/_4$ cups/300mL cream
3 egg yolks
2 tablespoons/25mL grated Gruyère cheese

METHOD

1. Wash and scrub the mussels well with a stiff brush. With a firm tug, pull the small piece of sea grass from the side of each mussel. Soak for 1 hour or so in water to allow the mussels to disgorge any sand.

2. Place the mussels in a large pan with the shallots and bay leaf, cover and cook over a brisk heat for 5 minutes or until the shells have opened. Remove with a slotted spoon. Taste the cooking juices and, if too salty, discard half.

3. Add the wine to the pan and reduce the liquid to about $^1/_2$ cup/125mL. Strain and reserve. Shell the mussels. If they are large discard the black rims, and set aside.

4. Wash, trim and slice the zucchini. Season with salt and pepper and sauté gently in the olive oil in a large frying pan until lightly browned. Transfer to a large gratin dish. Preheat the oven to 425°F/225°C.

5. Meanwhile, reduce 1 cup/250mL of the cream over a gentle heat to $^3/_4$ cup/175mL and stir in the reserved mussel cooking liquor. In a small bowl, beat the egg yolks with the remaining cream and stir in 2 tablespoons/25mL of the hot reduced cream mixture. Stir this mixture into the cream sauce in the pan, then remove from the heat. Check the seasoning.

6. Top the zucchini with the mussels then the cream sauce. Sprinkle with the cheese and heat in the preheated oven for 10 minutes, or until the top is browned.

MUSSEL AND ZUCCHINI GRATIN

Serves 6

Mussels in Shells with Herbed Mayonnaise

INGREDIENTS

Herbed Mayonnaise

1 large egg at room temperature
1¹/₂ tablespoons/20mL fresh lemon juice
1¹/₂ teaspoons/7mL Dijon-style mustard
1 cup/250mL olive oil
1 tablespoon/15mL tomato paste
2 cloves garlic, mashed to a paste
  with 1 teaspoon/5mL salt
pepper, to taste
¹/₃ cup/75mL chopped herbs: mostly
  parsley, some basil or oregano, a little
  thyme

3¹/₃lb/1¹/₂kg small mussels
6 green onions, chopped
2 bay leaves, crumbled
fresh basil leaves or chervil sprigs for
  garnish (optional)

METHOD

1. Make the mayonnaise. In a blender with the motor on high or in a food processor, blend the egg, lemon juice and mustard. Add the oil in a slow stream until a thick emulsion forms. Add the tomato paste, garlic and pepper to taste and blend the mayonnaise with the herbs until it is combined well. Transfer the mayonnaise to a small bowl. Cover and chill.

2. Scrub the mussels well in several changes of water, scrape off the beards and rinse the mussels. In a large pan, steam the mussels with 1 cup/250mL of water, the green onions and bay leaves, covered, over a moderately high heat for 5–7 minutes, or until the mussels are opened. Transfer them with a slotted spoon to a bowl, and discard any unopened mussels.

3. Remove the mussels from the shells, discarding half the shells, and arrange 1 mussel in each of the remaining shells.

4. Transfer the mussels to a large platter and chill them, covered, for 20 minutes. Just before serving, spoon about 1 teaspoon/5mL of the herb mayonnaise over each mussel and sprinkle the mussels with the basil or chervil, which should be finely shredded at the last moment.

Serves 4

Spaghetti Marinara

INGREDIENTS

1lb/500g spaghetti
2 teaspoons/10mL vegetable oil
2 teaspoons/10mL butter
2 onions, chopped
2 x 14oz/398mL canned tomatoes,
    undrained and mashed
2 tablespoons/25mL chopped fresh basil
    or 1 teaspoon/5mL dried basil
1/4 cup/60mL dry white wine
12 mussels, scrubbed and beards removed
12 scallops
12 uncooked prawns (shrimp),
    shelled and deveined
4oz/125g calamari (squid) rings

METHOD

1. Cook the pasta in boiling water in a large saucepan following the package directions. Drain, set aside and keep warm.

2. Heat the oil and butter in a frying pan over medium heat. Add the onions and cook, stirring, for 4 minutes or until the onions are golden.

3. Stir in the tomatoes, basil and wine and simmer for 8 minutes. Add the mussels, scallops and prawns (shrimp) and cook for 2 minutes longer.

4. Add the calamari (squid) and cook for 1 minute or until the shellfish is cooked. Spoon the seafood mixture over the hot pasta and serve immediately.

Serves 4

Clams in Sherry Sauce

INGREDIENTS

2 tablespoons/25mL olive oil
1 onion, finely chopped
2oz/50g cubed cured ham
2 tablespoons/25mL semi-sweet
    (oloroso) Spanish sherry
1 dozen very small clams

METHOD

1. Heat the oil in a small frying pan, sauté the onion for 1 minute, then cover and cook very slowly until the onion is tender but not colored (about 15 minutes). Stir in the ham, then add the sherry and the clams.

2. Turn the heat up to medium, cover and cook, removing the clams as they open. Return them to the sauce, making sure the clam meat is covered by the sauce. (May be prepared ahead.)

Serves 1

SPAGHETTI MARINARA

Mussels Mariniéres

INGREDIENTS

2lb/1kg mussels, cleaned

1 small onion, sliced

1 stalk celery, sliced

1 clove garlic, chopped

$1/4$ cup/50mL water or white wine

pepper

1 tablespoon/15mL butter

1 tablespoon/15mL parsley, chopped

METHOD

1. Place the mussels, onion, celery, garlic and water (or white wine) in a large saucepan.

2. Cook over medium heat until the mussels have opened. Stir frequently to ensure the mussels cook evenly.

3. Add pepper to taste. Stir in the butter and parsley just before serving.

Serves 3–4

Mussels Poulette

INGREDIENTS

2 tablespoons/25mL butter

1 onion, chopped

1½ cups/375mL mushrooms, sliced

2oz/50g bacon, diced

1 stalk celery, sliced

2lb/1kg mussels, cleaned

¼ cup/50mL white wine

1 cup/250mL Devon or whipping cream

METHOD

1. Place the butter, onion, mushrooms, bacon and celery in a saucepan over medium heat. Cook for 3 minutes.

2. Add the mussels and white wine. Cook until the mussels are opened, stirring frequently.

3. Stir in the cream and cook for a further minute. Serve immediately.

Serves 3–4

Clams with Pasta

INGREDIENTS

2 tablespoons/25mL olive oil

1 large onion, finely chopped

1 clove garlic, minced

1 red bell pepper, finely chopped

1 medium tomato, skinned, seeded
   and finely chopped

1 tablespoon/15mL chopped parsley

1 bay leaf

few strands of saffron

salt and freshly ground pepper

8oz/250g spaghetti, broken into
   3 lengths

¾ cup/175mL veal broth, or a
   mixture of chicken and beef broth

2 dozen very small clams

3 tablespoons/45mL fresh or
   frozen peas

salt and pepper

METHOD

1. Heat 1 tablespoon/15mL of the oil in a frying pan. Sauté the onion, garlic and red bell pepper for 1 minute, then cover and cook slowly until the vegetables are tender but not brown (about 20 minutes). Add the tomato, parsley, bay leaf, saffron, salt and pepper to the onion mixture and cook for 5 minutes, uncovered.

2. Meanwhile, bring a large pot of salted water to the boil with the remaining oil. Add the spaghetti and cook, stirring occasionally. Drain the spaghetti and return to the pot. Combine the onion and tomato mixture in the pot with the spaghetti, add ½ cup/120mL of the broth, along with the clams and the peas. Mix well. Cover and continue cooking until the clams have opened (about 10 minutes).

3. To serve, add the remaining broth (the mixture should be a little soupy) and season with salt and pepper – it should be well seasoned. Serve in small individual casserole dishes. Although best prepared at the last minute, this dish can be made in advance and reheated.

Serves 2

Mussels Provençal

INGREDIENTS

1 tablespoon/15mL olive oil
1/2 red bell pepper, chopped
2 tomatoes, roughly chopped
1 clove garlic, chopped
1 stalk celery, sliced
1 onion, chopped
2lb/1kg mussels, cleaned
3 tablespoons/45mL white wine
1 tablespoon/15mL chopped basil

METHOD

1. Place the oil, bell pepper, tomatoes, garlic, celery and onion in a saucepan over medium heat. Cook for 4 minutes.

2. Add the mussels and white wine. Cook until the mussels are opened, stirring frequently.

3. Stir in the basil just before serving.

Serves 2

Mussels in Vinaigrette

INGREDIENTS

4 1/2lb/2kg mussels
salt

Vinaigrette Sauce
1/3 cup/75mL olive oil
3 tablespoons/45mL wine vinegar
2 tablespoons/25mL finely chopped onion
2 tablespoons/25mL finely chopped canned
   or homemade sweet red bell peppers
1 tablespoon/15mL finely chopped parsley
salt and pepper

METHOD

1. Scrub and scrape the mussels well and remove the beards. Throw away any mussels that are open and do not close when tapped with a knife. Wash well in water and drain.

2. Place the mussels in a saucepan with 1 cup/250mL of cold water and a pinch of salt. Place over high heat, cover and bring to the boil. Remove the mussels as they open and leave to cool. Throw away any that do not open.

3. Make the vinaigrette sauce by mixing the oil, vinegar, onion, sweet red bell pepper, parsley and some salt and pepper in a bowl. Arrange the mussels in a dish and spoon the sauce over each one.

Serves 6–8

MUSSELS PROVENÇAL

Mussels with Herbed Garlic Butter

INGREDIENTS

2lb/1kg mussels
1/3 cup/75mL butter
2 cloves garlic, peeled and crushed
2 tablespoons/25mL finely chopped basil
1/2 bunch finely chopped parsley
steamed rice or noodles

METHOD

1. Remove the fibrous beards from the mussels by pulling firmly. Wash the mussels well, scrubbing with a small brush if necessary.

2. Combine the butter, garlic, basil and parsley. This can be done in a food processor.

3. Place the mussels in a heavy-based frying pan over a medium heat.

4. As the mussels start to open, spoon the herb butter over and into the mussels, continuing to add butter until all has been used. Serve on individual plates over steamed rice or noodles, which take on the delicious juices.

Serves 4

Spaghetti Vongole

INGREDIENTS

10oz/285g spaghetti

3 tablespoons/45mL virgin olive oil

1 onion, very finely chopped

2 cloves garlic, finely chopped

1lb/500g clams, cleaned and sand removed

$1/2$ cup/125mL white wine

salt and pepper

1 tablespoon/15mL fresh chopped oregano

METHOD

1. Pre-cook the spaghetti in boiling water. Refresh in cold water, stir with half the oil and set aside.

2. Heat the remaining oil in a large cooking pot over high heat. Add the onion, garlic and cook for 1 minute.

3. Add the clams, white wine, salt and pepper.

4. When all the clams have opened, add the spaghetti and oregano. Cook for another 2 minutes and serve.

Serves 3–4

Clams in Spicy Tomato Sauce

INGREDIENTS

1 onion

2 cloves garlic, minced

2 tablespoons/25mL olive oil

2 tomatoes, peeled and chopped

1 tablespoon/15mL tomato paste

1 teaspoon/5mL paprika

$1/2$ cup/125mL dry white wine

salt and freshly ground pepper

1 tablespoon/15mL chopped parsley

$1/2$ dried red chili, seeds removed,
    crumbled

18 very small clams

METHOD

1. In a shallow casserole or cooking pot, sauté the onion and garlic in the oil until the onion is wilted. Add the tomatoes, tomato paste, paprika, wine, salt, pepper, parsley and chili. Cover and cook for 10 minutes. Add the clams, cover tightly and cook over a high heat until the clams open. Serve in the same dish.

Serves 4–6

SPAGHETTI VONGOLE

LIGHT MEALS

Spaghetti with Mussels

INGREDIENTS

8oz/250g spaghetti

1/2 cup/125mL olive oil

1 onion, finely chopped

3 cloves garlic, finely chopped

4 vine-ripened tomatoes, diced finely

1lb/500g mussels, cleaned

1 tablespoon/15mL fresh aromatic
    herbs, chopped

1/2 cup/125mL dry white wine

salt and pepper to taste

2 tablespoons/25mL grated
    Parmesan cheese

1 tablespoon/15mL chopped parsley

METHOD

1. Pre-cook the spaghetti in water. Refresh in cold water after cooking and toss with half the oil. Set aside.

2. Heat the remaining oil over a high heat in a large pot. Add the onion, garlic and tomatoes and cook for 10 minutes.

3. Add the mussels, chopped herbs, white wine and salt and pepper.

4. When the mussels start to open add the spaghetti.

5. Stir together until all the mussels have opened.

6. Serve with the Parmesan and parsley sprinkled on top.

Serves 4

Baked Stuffed Clams

INGREDIENTS

18 clams

1 tablespoon/15mL olive oil

2 tablespoons/25mL minced onion

1 clove garlic, minced

6 tablespoons/90mL breadcrumbs

2 tablespoons/25mL minced cured ham

1 tablespoon/15mL dry sherry

1/4 teaspoon/1mL lemon juice

salt and pepper

1/4 teaspoon/1mL paprika

1 tablespoon/15mL minced parsley

butter

METHOD

1. Open the clams with a knife. Chop the meat and reserve half the shells.

2. In a small frying pan, heat the oil and sauté the onion and garlic until the onion is wilted. Stir in the breadcrumbs, ham, sherry, lemon juice, a little salt and pepper, paprika and parsley. Mix in the clam meat. Stuff the reserved shells with the filling.

3. Dot with butter and bake in oven at 350°F/180°C for about 10 minutes, or until slightly browned.

Serves 4–6

Mediterranean Fish Stew

INGREDIENTS

Rouille

2 cloves garlic, chopped

1 small red chili, deseeded
   and chopped

3 tablespoons/45mL chopped fresh
   cilantro

pinch of salt

3 tablespoons/45mL mayonnaise

1 tablespoon/15mL olive oil

2lb/1kg mixed fish and shellfish, such as
   cod or snapper fillet, raw prawns (shrimp)
   with shells intact and calamari (squid)
   tubes

1lb/500g mussels, cleaned

2 tablespoons/25mL olive oil

1 onion, finely chopped

1 teaspoon/5mL fennel seeds

1 cup/250mL dry white wine

14oz/398mL can chopped tomatoes

salt and pepper to taste

METHOD

1. First make the rouille. Crush together the garlic, chili, cilantro and a pinch of salt with a pestle and mortar. Stir in the mayonnaise and oil, mix well and season to taste. Refrigerate until needed.

2. Skin the fish, if necessary, and cut into 2in/5cm chunks. Shell the prawns (shrimp), then slit open the back of each one and scrape out any black vein. Rinse well. Cut the calamari (squid) into 2in/5cm rings. Shell the mussels, reserving a few with shells on to garnish.

3. Heat the oil in a large heavy-based saucepan and fry the onion for 4 minutes to soften. Add the fennel seeds and fry for another minute, then add the wine, tomatoes and seasoning. Bring to the boil, then simmer, uncovered, for 5 minutes, until slightly thickened. Add the fish, calamari (squid), mussels and prawns and simmer, covered, for a further 5–6 minutes, stirring occasionally, until the prawns (shrimp) are pink and everything is cooked. Season and serve with the rouille.

Serves 6–8

Seafood Paella

INGREDIENTS

1 tablespoon/15mL olive oil

2 onions, chopped

2 cloves garlic, crushed

1 tablespoon/15mL fresh thyme leaves

2 teaspoons/10mL finely grated lemon rind

4 ripe tomatoes, chopped

2$^{1}/_{2}$ cups/625mL short-grain white rice

pinch saffron threads soaked in
  2 cups/500mL water

5 cups/1.25L chicken or fish stock

2$^{1}/_{2}$ cups/625mL fresh or frozen peas

2 red bell peppers, chopped

2lb/1kg mussels, scrubbed and
  beards removed

1lb/500g firm white fish fillets, chopped

10oz/285g peeled uncooked prawns
  (shrimp)

8oz/250g scallops

3 calamari (squid) tubes, sliced

1 tablespoon/15mL chopped fresh parsley

METHOD

1. Preheat the barbecue to a medium heat. Place a large paella or frying pan on the barbecue, add the oil and heat. Add the onions, garlic, thyme leaves and lemon rind and cook for 3 minutes or until the onion is soft.

2. Add the tomatoes and cook, stirring, for 4 minutes. Add the rice and cook, stirring, for 4 minutes longer or until the rice is translucent. Stir in the saffron mixture and stock and bring to a simmer. Simmer, stirring occasionally, for 30 minutes or until the rice has absorbed almost all of the liquid. Stir in the peas, bell pepper and mussels and cook for 2 minutes. Add the fish, prawns (shrimp) and scallops and cook, stirring, for 2–3 minutes. Stir in calamari (squid) and parsley and cook, stirring, for 1–2 minutes longer or until the seafood is cooked.

Serves 8

Fried Mussels

INGREDIENTS

2 eggs, lightly beaten

salt and pepper

2 cups/500mL breadcrumbs

1 tablespoon/15mL dry mixed
   aromatic herbs

2lb/1kg black mussels cleaned, cooked
   mariniéres style and removed from the
   shell (see page 48)

oil for deep frying

3 tablespoons/45mL tartar sauce

METHOD

1. Place the eggs in a bowl and season with a little salt and pepper.

2. Combine the breadcrumbs and herbs in a separate bowl.

3. Dip the mussels in the egg mixture, then roll in breadcrumbs.

4. Deep-fry the mussels in hot oil, until golden brown.

5. Drain on paper towels and serve immediately with tartar sauce.

Serves 4

FRIED MUSSELS

LEMON-SCENTED FISH PIE

Lemon-Scented Fish Pie

INGREDIENTS

2lb/1kg potatoes, cut into even-sized pieces (6 medium)

salt and black pepper

$1/4$ cup/50mL butter

1 onion, chopped

2 stalks celery, sliced

2 tablespoons/25mL all-purpose flour

1 cup/250mL fish stock

finely grated rind and juice of 1 large lemon

1lb/500g white fish, cut into cubes

6oz/175g cooked and shelled mussels

2 tablespoons/25mL chopped fresh parsley

4 tablespoons/60mL milk

METHOD

1. Cook the potatoes in boiling salted water for 15–20 minutes, until tender, then drain.

2. Meanwhile, melt half of the butter in a large saucepan, then add the onion and celery and cook for 2–3 minutes, until softened. Add the flour and cook, stirring, for 1 minute, then slowly add the fish stock and cook, stirring, until thickened. Add the lemon rind and juice and season with pepper.

3. Preheat the oven to 425°F/220°C. Remove the sauce from the heat, stir in the fish, mussels and parsley, then transfer to an oven-proof dish. Mash the potatoes with the remaining butter and the milk. Season, then spread evenly over the fish with a fork. Cook in the oven for 30–40 minutes, until the sauce is bubbling and the topping is starting to brown.

Serves 4

Chili-Spiked Mussels in Spaghetti

INGREDIENTS

12oz/375g dried spaghetti

2lb/1kg fresh mussels

2 tablespoons/25mL olive oil, plus 1 tablespoon/15mL
extra for drizzling

2 shallots, finely chopped

4 cloves garlic, chopped

2/3 cup/150mL dry white wine

grated rind of 1 lemon

1 teaspoon/5mL dried chili flakes

2 tablespoons/25mL chopped fresh parsley

black pepper, to taste

METHOD

1. Cook the pasta according to the package instructions, until tender but still
firm to the bite, then drain well. Meanwhile, scrub the mussels under cold running
water, pull away any beards and discard any mussels that are open or damaged.

2. Place the mussels in a large heavy-based saucepan, with just the water clinging
to the shells. Steam for 3–4 minutes over a high heat, shaking regularly, until the
shells have opened. Discard any mussels that remain closed.

3. Heat 2 tablespoons/25mL of oil in a large saucepan and gently fry the shallots
and garlic for 5 minutes or until softened. Add the wine and boil rapidly for
5–6 minutes, until the liquid has reduced by half. Add the mussels, lemon rind
and chili and heat for 2–3 minutes. Add the pasta to the mussels, then stir in
the parsley and black pepper. Gently toss over heat and drizzle remaining
oil over.

Serves 4

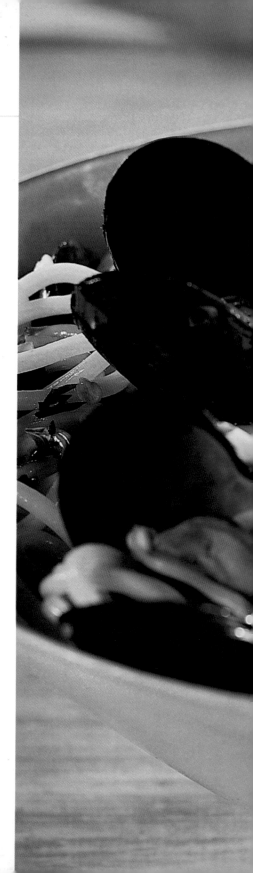

Belgian-Style Mussels

INGREDIENTS

4 1/2 lb/2kg mussels in their shells

2 tablespoons/25mL butter

1 tablespoon/15mL vegetable oil

4 shallots or 1 onion, chopped

2 stalks celery, chopped, plus any leaves

2/3 cup/150mL dry white wine

black pepper

2/3 cup/150mL Devon or whipping cream

4 tablespoons/60mL chopped fresh
   flat-leaf Italian parsley

METHOD

1. Scrub the mussels under cold running water, then pull away any beards and discard any mussels that are open or damaged. Heat the butter and oil in a very large saucepan, then add the shallots or onion and celery (reserving leaves) and cook for 2–3 minutes, until the shallots or onion are translucent.

2. Stir in the wine and plenty of pepper and bring to the boil. Add the mussels, cover and cook over a high heat, shaking the pan occasionally, for 4–5 minutes, until the mussels have opened. Remove from the pan and keep warm in a bowl, discarding any that remain closed.

3. Roughly chop the celery leaves, reserving a few for garnish. Add the chopped leaves, cream and parsley to the cooking juices and season again if necessary. Bring to the boil, then spoon over the mussels. Garnish with celery leaves.

Serves 4

Marinated Mussels

INGREDIENTS

Marinade
1/2 cup/125mL olive oil
3 tablespoons/45mL red wine vinegar
1 teaspoon/5mL small capers
1 tablespoon/15mL minced onion
1 tablespoon/15mL minced pimiento
  (Spanish red peppers, homemade
  or imported)
1 tablespoon/15mL chopped parsley
salt and pepper

2 dozen medium mussels
1 cup/250mL water
1 slice lemon

METHOD

1. Mix the oil, vinegar, capers, onion, pimiento, parsley, salt and pepper in a bowl and set aside. Scrub the mussels well, removing the beards. Discard any that do not close tightly.

2. Place the water in a saucepan with the lemon slice. Add the mussels and bring to the boil. Remove the mussels as they open, then cool.

3. Remove the mussel meat from the shells and add to the bowl with the marinade.

4. Cover and refrigerate overnight. Reserve half the mussel shells, clean them well, and place them in a plastic bag in the refrigerator. Before serving, replace the mussels in their shells and spoon a small amount of the marinade over each.

Serves 4–6

Mussels in Parsley Sauce

INGREDIENTS

2 tablespoons/25mL olive oil
1 small onion, finely chopped
2 cloves garlic, minced
1 teaspoon/5mL all-purpose flour
1/2 cup/125mL dry white wine
1 bay leaf
2 tablespoons/25mL fresh lemon juice
freshly ground pepper
salt
2 dozen medium mussels
1 tablespoon/15mL minced parsley

METHOD

1. Heat the oil in a shallow casserole, preferably Spanish earthenware. Sauté the onion and garlic until the onion is wilted. Stir in the flour and cook for 1 minute. Add the wine, bay leaf, lemon juice, pepper and a little salt. Simmer, covered, for 5 minutes. (May be prepared ahead.)

2. Add the mussels to the sauce, cover and cook until the mussels have opened. Sprinkle with the parsley and serve.

Serves 2

ENTERTAINING

Bouillabaisse

INGREDIENTS

6¹/2lb/3kg fish heads and bones
4 tablespoons/60mL olive oil
3 cups/750mL dry white wine
4 carrots, peeled and sliced
2 leeks, washed and sliced
2 onions, peeled and sliced
3 stalks celery, sliced
6 tomatoes, chopped
1 teaspoon/5mL peppercorns
1 bunch thyme, tied together
1 bunch parsley, tied together
1 bunch dill, tied together
4 fresh bay leaves
12 cups/3L of water
salt and pepper

Soup
2 tablespoons/25mL olive oil
2 large leeks, washed and sliced
1 large fennel bulb, finely sliced
6 shallots, peeled and sliced
3 medium potatoes, peeled and diced
large pinch of saffron threads
2 x 14oz/398g cans Italian-style tomatoes
4¹/2lb/2kg assorted fish fillets, diced
20oz/570g large prawns (shrimp), peeled
2¹/4lb/1kg mussels, scrubbed and rinsed
18oz/510g small calamari (squid), cleaned
1 bunch parsley, chopped
1 loaf sourdough bread
salt and pepper, to taste

For the Rouille
2 large red bell peppers
1 cup/250mL breadcrumbs
3 cloves garlic
1 teaspoon/5mL red wine vinegar
1 cup/250mL liquid from soup
2 small red chilies
olive oil
salt and pepper

METHOD

1. Rinse the fish heads and bones and set aside. Heat the olive oil in a deep saucepan and add the fish heads and bones. Cook the fish pieces over a high heat, stirring constantly, until the fish pieces begin to break down, scraping up anything that sticks to the bottom of the pan, (for about 20 minutes). Add the wine and simmer, stirring well. Add the prepared vegetables, herbs, bay leaves and water and simmer for 30 minutes, skimming any scum off the surface as it appears. After 30 minutes, strain the stock thoroughly, pressing on the solids to extract as much liquid as possible. Return to the heat for a further 20 minutes then add salt and pepper to taste. Set aside.

2. To make the soup, heat the olive oil in a saucepan and add the sliced leeks, fennel, shallots, potatoes and saffron and cook over medium heat until all the vegetables are golden and soft (about 20 minutes).

Add the squashed canned tomatoes and reserved fish stock and bring the soup to the boil. Add salt and pepper to taste.

3. Add the fish, prawns (shrimp) and mussels and simmer for 10 minutes. Add the calamari (squid) and parsley and stir gently. Remove the soup from the heat and cover. Allow to rest for 10 minutes. Meanwhile, brush the sliced sourdough bread with olive oil and grill until golden on both sides. Rub a clove of garlic over each golden slice. To serve, place a slice of grilled bread on the bottom of each soup bowl and ladle the hot soup over, making sure that everyone gets some mussels, prawns (shrimp) and calamari (squid). Add a spoonful of rouille if desired.

4. To make the rouille, roast and then skin the bell peppers under a hot grill. Then place peppers, breadcrumbs, garlic, vinegar, soup liquid and chilies in a food processor and process. Be careful not to over-process. When the ingredients are well mixed add enough olive oil and salt and pepper to make a flavorful paste.

Serves 10–12

Oysters and Mussels in Shells

INGREDIENTS

1lb/500g mussels, scrubbed and
    beards removed
24 oysters in half shells
1/4 cup/50mL butter, softened
1 tablespoon/15mL chopped fresh parsley
2 tablespoons/25mL lemon juice
1 tablespoon/15mL orange juice
1 tablespoon/15mL white wine

METHOD

1. Preheat a barbecue to a high heat. Place the mussels and oysters on the barbecue grill and cook for 3–5 minutes or until the mussel shells open and the oysters are warm. Discard any mussels that do not open after 5 minutes of cooking.

2. Place the butter, parsley, lemon juice, orange juice and wine in a heavy-based saucepan. Place on the barbecue and cook, stirring, for 2 minutes or until the mixture is bubbling. Place the mussels and oysters on serving platter, drizzle with the butter mixture and serve immediately.

Serves 6

Clams in Romesco Sauce

INGREDIENTS

2 dozen very small clams
water, salt and cornmeal for soaking
2 pimientos, homemade or imported,
    cut into strips
1/2 cup/125mL red wine vinegar
1 bay leaf

Fish Broth
1 small whole white fish, head on, cleaned
1/4 cup/50mL dry white wine
11/2 cups/375mL water
1/2 bay leaf
1/4 teaspoon/1mL thyme
1 small onion
1 small carrot, peeled and cut in half
6 peppercorns
salt

3 tablespoons/45mL olive oil
2 slices French-style bread

3 cloves garlic, peeled
12 blanched almonds
1/2 cup/125mL dry white wine
1 dried red chili, seeds removed and
    chopped
salt
freshly ground pepper
1 teaspoon/5mL grappa (optional)
1 tablespoon/15mL chopped parsley

METHOD

1. Scrub the clams well and soak overnight in water, salt, and cornmeal to rid the clams of any sand. Soak the pimientos in a bowl with the vinegar and bay leaf for 3–4 hours.

2. To make the broth, place all broth ingredients in a saucepan and bring to the boil. Cover and simmer for 1 hour. Strain and reserve 1 cup/250mL. Drain the pimientos, and dry them on paper towels. Heat the oil in a large, shallow casserole. Sauté the pimientos about 2 minutes. Transfer them to a blender or processor, leaving the remaining oil in the pan. Fry the bread slices and garlic in the remaining oil, until both are golden. Add them to the blender, along with the almonds. Blend until a paste forms. With the motor running, add 1/4 cup/50mL of the fish broth. When it is well blended, add the remaining broth and the wine. Beat until smooth.

3. Heat the saucepan again. Strain the contents of the blender into the pan and add the chili, salt and pepper. Arrange the clams in the pan, cover and cook over a medium flame, removing the clams as they open. Correct the seasoning and remove the saucepan from the heat. Stir in the grappa (if desired) and return the clams to the pan, making sure that the shell section with the clam meat is covered by the sauce. Cover and set aside for 1–2 hours. Reheat and serve, sprinkled with the parsley.

Serves 4–6

ENTERTAINING

Mussel Shooters

INGREDIENTS

Bloody Mary Mix
1 cup/250mL tomato juice
1/4 cup/50mL vodka
a few drops of Worcestershire sauce
a few drops of Tabasco sauce
celery salt and pepper

18 mussels, cooked mariniéres style, taken
   out of the shell (see page 48)
chives, finely chopped (optional)
freshly ground black pepper (optional)
lemon slices and baby dill pickles (optional)

METHOD

1. Combine all the Bloody Mary ingredients and
stir until combined. Refrigerate for 2–3 hours.

2. Take 6 shooter glasses and add 3 mussels to
each glass. Top the glasses with Bloody Mary
mix, garnish with chives, black pepper, lemon
slices and dill pickles (optional), and serve
immediately.

Serves 6

Crispy Baked Mussels

INGREDIENTS

24 mussels, cooked mariniéres style, top
   shell removed (see page 48)
4oz/125g bacon, partially cooked,
   chopped
1/3 cup/75mL butter
2 green onions, chopped
1/2 cup/125mL soft breadcrumbs
2 tablespoons/25mL freshly squeezed
   lemon juice
salt and pepper
chopped chives, for garnish

METHOD

1. Line a baking dish large enough to hold the
mussels in one layer with crumpled foil. Add the
mussels. The foil will keep the mussels upright.
Scatter the bacon over the mussels.

2. Melt the butter in a small frying pan, add the
green onions. Sauté until soft. Add the
breadcrumbs and lemon juice and cook until the
breadcrumbs are starting to crisp. Season with
salt and pepper.

3. Spoon the breadcrumb mixture over mussels.
Bake in a 400°F/200°C oven until the mussels
are heated through and the tops are crisp. Serve
hot, garnished with chives.

Makes 24

Moules Mernier

INGREDIENTS

4 1/2 lb/2kg fresh mussels

2 onions, chopped

3 shallots, chopped

2 tablespoons/25mL chopped fresh
   parsley, plus extra to garnish

2/3 cup/150mL water

2/3 cup/150mL white wine or
   fish stock

4 tablespoons/60mL whipping cream

salt and black pepper

METHOD

1. Scrub the mussels under cold running water, then pull away any beards and discard any mussels that are open or damaged.

2. Place the onions, shallots, parsley, water, and the wine or stock in a large heavy-based saucepan. Cook gently for 10 minutes or until the onions and shallots have softened. Add the mussels, then cover and cook for 5 minutes or until the shells have opened, shaking the pan from time to time. Place a colander over a bowl and strain the mussels. Reserve the cooking liquid and discard any mussels that remain closed.

3. Pour the reserved liquid into the pan and boil for 5 minutes or until reduced by half. Remove from the heat and stir in the cream. Season, if necessary. Return to the heat and warm through, but do not boil. Divide the mussels among 4 large bowls, pour over the sauce and sprinkle with parsley.

Serves 4

Mussel Salsa

INGREDIENTS

1 1/2 cups/375mL/13oz marinated
   green shelled mussels, drained

1/4 cup/50mL lime juice

1 teaspoon/5mL garlic, crushed

1/2 red onion, diced

1 ripe tomato, diced

small bunch cilantro, chopped

6–10 drops Tabasco sauce, depending
   on taste

salt and freshly ground black pepper,
   to taste

1 package crackers

METHOD

1. In a medium-sized bowl, combine all of the ingredients except crackers and mix well

2. Serve with crackers.

Serves 4

MOULES MERNIER

Escargot Mussels

INGREDIENTS

**2lb/1kg mussels, cooked mariniéres
style (see page 48)**

Garlic Butter
1lb/500g softened butter
2 cloves garlic, minced
1 tablespoon/15mL chopped fresh parsley
2 tablespoons/30mL brandy
salt and pepper

METHOD

1. Remove the extra half shells and keep the mussels in one shell.

2. To make garlic butter, combine all the ingredients in a bowl and mix well.

3. Top up the half shell mussels with garlic butter.

4. Grill the mussels until sizzling and serve with bread.

Serves 4

ESCARGOT MUSSELS

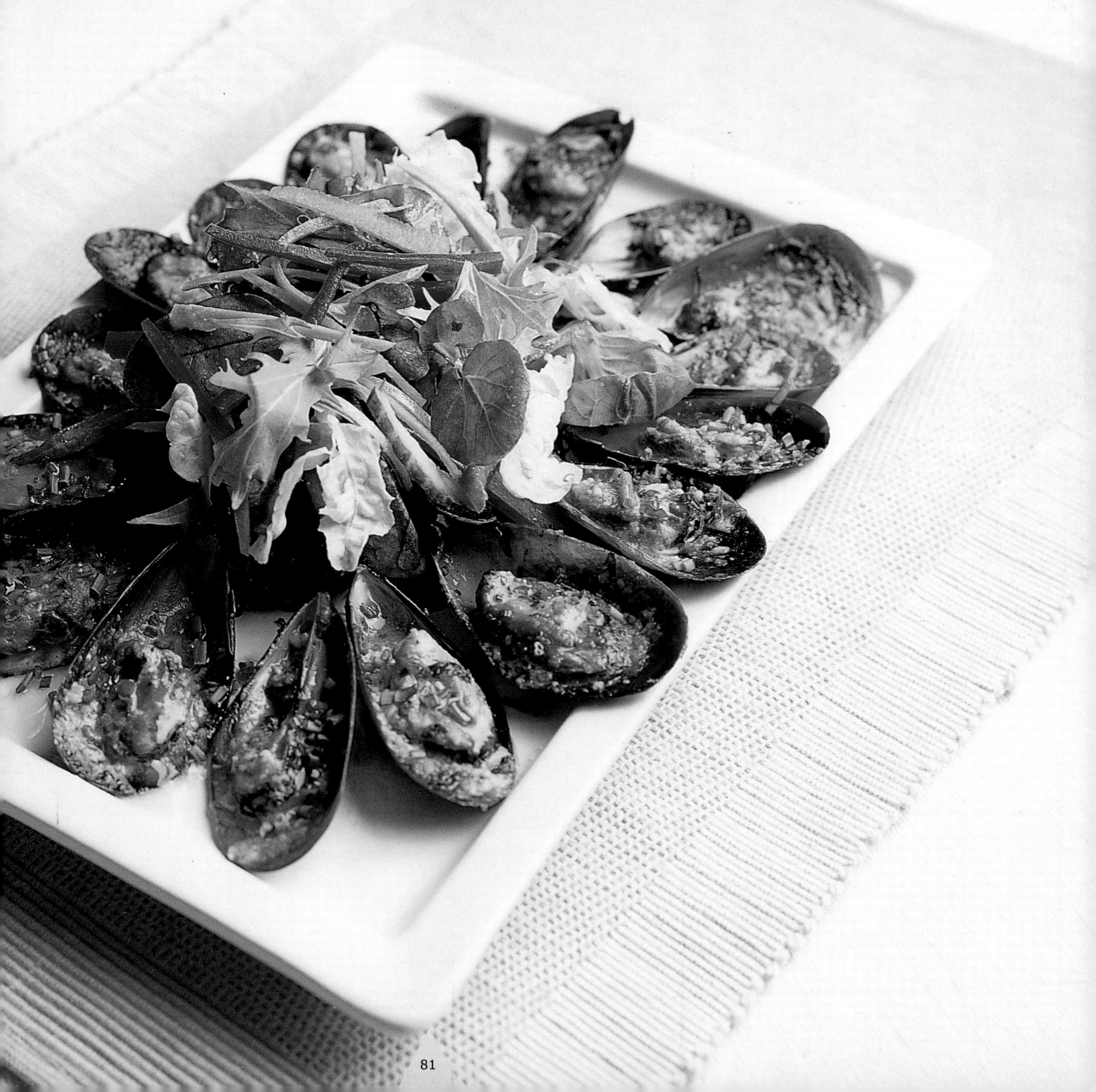

Mussels in White Wine with Garlic, Onions and Tomatoes

INGREDIENTS

1 hard-boiled egg

2 tablespoons/25mL olive oil

1 small onion, finely chopped

1 clove garlic, crushed

1/4 cup/50mL fresh breadcrumbs

1 cup/250mL canned peeled tomato pieces,
    finely chopped

24 mussels or clams, bearded
    and scrubbed

1 1/2 cups/375mL dry white wine

1 bay leaf

salt and pepper

2 tablespoons/25mL finely chopped parsley

1 lemon

METHOD

1. Sieve the hard-boiled egg yolk and finely chop the white.

2. Heat the oil in a small frying pan, add the onion and garlic and sauté until the onion is soft but not brown (about 5 minutes).

3. Stir in the breadcrumbs, tomatoes and sieved egg yolk. Cook while stirring until most of the liquid has evaporated and the mixture is a purée. Reserve.

4. Place the mussels in a large saucepan, add the wine and bay leaf and bring to the boil.

Cover, reduce heat to very low and simmer for 8–10 minutes. Remove the mussels with a slotted spoon to a warm serving dish. Discard any unopened mussels.

5. Strain the mussel liquid into the tomato mixture. Stir and bring to the boil. Add salt and pepper to taste. Pour the sauce over the mussels, sprinkle with the chopped egg white and parsley. Cut the lemon into wedges or slices and use as garnish. Serve with crusty bread.

Serves 4

Béchamel-Coated Mussels with Cured Ham

INGREDIENTS

18 fresh medium-sized mussels

1/4 cup/50mL water

1/4 cup/50mL dry white wine

1 bay leaf

White Sauce

5 tablespoons/75mL unsalted butter

6 tablespoons/90mL all-purpose flour

3/4 cup/175mL milk

salt and freshly ground pepper

dash of nutmeg

3oz/75g cured ham, in very thin slices

1/2 cup/125mL fresh breadcrumbs

1 tablespoon/15mL grated cheese, such as
    Manchego or Parmesan

2 eggs, lightly beaten

oil for frying

METHOD

1. Place the mussels in a saucepan with the water, wine and bay leaf. Bring to the boil, reduce the heat to medium, cover and cook, removing the mussels as they open. Transfer the cooking liquid to a bowl, remove the mussel shells and place the mussels in the liquid until ready to use. Drain the liquid from the mussels, reserving 3/4 cup/175mL (if there is less, add a little water).

2. To make the white sauce, melt the butter in a saucepan. Add the flour and cook, stirring, for a minute or two. Stir in the reserved mussel broth, the milk, salt, pepper and nutmeg, and cook stirring

constantly, until the sauce reaches boiling point. Turn off the heat and stir the sauce occasionally until ready to use. Dry the mussels well on paper towels. Wrap a piece of ham, of about the width of a mussel, around each mussel. Coat with the white sauce and place on a dish. Refrigerate for at least 1 hour, or until the sauce becomes firm. (May be prepared ahead.)

3. Combine the breadcrumbs with the grated cheese. Coat the mussels with the beaten egg, then cover with breadcrumbs. Refrigerate. In a saucepan heat the oil at least 1/2in/1cm deep to about 380°F/195°C and fry the mussels quickly until golden. Or, better, use a deep-fryer. Drain.

Serves 4

Mussel Crêpes

INGREDIENTS

4¹/2 lb/2kg mussels

¹/2 cup/125mL dry white wine

2 tablespoons/25mL chopped onion

4 parsley stalks, bruised

5 black peppercorns, crushed

Crêpes

⁷/8 cup/100g all-purpose flour

2 large eggs

mussel broth (see method)

4–6 tablespoons/60-90mL Devon or
    whipping cream

4 tablespoons/60mL butter

6 tablespoons/90mL fresh parsley, chopped

METHOD

1. Wash the mussels, discarding any that are open (and do not close when touched). Pull off the beards. Place the wine, onion, parsley stalks and peppercorns in a large pan and bring to a simmer.

2. Add the mussels (in 2 batches) and cover. Cook over high heat for 3–4 minutes, shaking occasionally, until they are open.

3. Discard the shells and any that remain shut. Strain the liquid and leave to cool. Taste for seasoning. Make the crêpe batter. Place the flour in a bowl or blender and work in the eggs, mussel liquid and 2 tablespoons/25mL of cream. (Don't overbeat in a blender.) Allow to stand for 1 hour.

4. Melt 1 tablespoon/15mL of butter in a frying pan, swirling it around. Add to the batter and stir thoroughly. To cook crêpes, heat another tablespoon/15mL of butter and swirl. Use about ³/4 cup/175mL crêpe batter per crêpe. It is easiest to pour from a cup.

5. Lift the pan and pour the batter fast into the middle of the pan and in a circle around, tilting the pan to cover the base. (If you overdo the liquid, spoon off anything that doesn't set at once. Crêpes should be thin.)

6. Return the pan to the heat, shaking it to make sure the crêpe does not stick. Cook for 1 minute until golden underneath, then flip over using a spatula. Briefly cook the other side. Roll and keep warm on a plate while you make more.

7. Warm the remaining cream in a saucepan with the mussel bodies. Spoon the mussels and a little cream onto one edge of a crêpe, sprinkle with parsley and roll up. Garnish with any remaining cream and a sprinkle of parsley. Serve immediately

Serves 6

MUSSEL CREPES

Mussels Ardennais

INGREDIENTS

12 large mussels
1 tablespoon/15mL butter
1 French shallot, chopped
1 large vine-ripened tomato, diced finely
thyme
salt and pepper
12 small slices of Ardenne ham or Black
  Forest ham
2oz/50g Emmental or vintage Cheddar
  cheese, grated

METHOD

1. Cook the mussels mariniéres style (see page 46), remove from the shell and set aside, retaining half of the shells.

2. Place the butter, shallot, tomato and thyme in a pot and cook over medium heat for 10 minutes. Season with salt and pepper.

3. Place the mixture in the base of the half shells.

4. Roll the mussels in the ham and place o top of the mixture in the mussel shells.

5. Sprinkle with cheese and warm under th grill until the cheese has melted.

Makes 12

Tuna-Stuffed Mussels

INGREDIENTS

1 small can flaked tuna in oil
  (reserve the oil)
2 teaspoons/10mL red wine vinegar
4 teaspoons/20mL minced shallots
2 teaspoons/10mL minced parsley
18 large mussels
1 cup/250mL water
1 slice lemon
2 hard-boiled egg yolks
flour, for dusting
1 egg, lightly beaten
breadcrumbs
oil, for frying

METHOD

1. In a cup, combine 2 tablespoons/25mL of the tuna oil, the vinegar, shallots and parsley.

2. Place the mussels in a frying pan with the water and the lemon slice. Bring to a boil and remove the mussels as they open. Discard any that do not open. Remove the mussel meat and discard the shells.

3. In a small bowl mash together the egg yolks and tuna. Fill each mussel with about 1 teaspoon/5mL of this mixture (the mussels have an opening into which you place the filling). Dust with flour, cover with the beaten egg, and coat with the breadcrumbs. (May be prepared ahead.)

4. In a frying pan, deep-fry the mussels until golden brown. Drain on paper towels.

5. Drizzle the oil and vinegar mixture over the mussels and serve warm.

Serves 3–4

Mussels Florentine

INGREDIENTS

Mousseline Sauce
4 egg yolks
4 tablespoons/60mL water
2 tablespoons/25mL melted butter
salt, pepper and nutmeg
1 lemon, juiced
1 tablespoon/15mL whipping cream

2lb/1kg mussels, cooked mariniéres
style and divided in half shells
(see page 48)
small bunch (about 4 cups/1L) fresh
spinach, cooked and chopped, mixed
with 2 tablespoons/25mL
melted butter

METHOD

1. To make the mousseline sauce, whisk the egg yolks and water together in a double boiler until a light mayonnaise consistency.

2. Add the melted butter little by little, whisking vigorously, then season and add the lemon juice.

3. Add the whipped cream, and set aside (keep warm).

4. Take the cooked mussels out of the shell.

5. Warm the spinach in a pot and fill each mussel shell with warm spinach.

6. Put the mussels back on the bed of spinach.

7. Place the mousseline sauce over the mussels.

8. Grill until golden brown and serve.

Serves 4

Clams with Mushrooms and Cured Ham

INGREDIENTS

3 tablespoons/45mL olive oil
1 1/2 cups/375mL mushrooms, halved
or quartered
2 cloves garlic, sliced
6 tablespoons/90mL veal broth, or a
mixture of chicken and beef broth
2 tablespoons/25mL diced cured ham,
cut from a 1/2in/1cm thick slice
1 teaspoon/5mL fresh lemon juice
1/2 teaspoon/2mL chili powder
1 bay leaf
1lb/500g clams in the shell
1 tablespoon/15mL minced parsley

METHOD

1. Heat the oil in a frying pan and sauté the mushrooms and garlic for about 2 minutes. Remove to a warm platter. Add the broth, ham, lemon juice, chili powder, bay leaf and clams. Cover and cook, removing the clams as they open. Return the clams to the casserole, making sure the clam meat is covered by the sauce. (May be prepared ahead.) Sprinkle with parsley and serve in the same dish.

Serves 2

MUSSELS FLORENTINE

Mussels in Pernod Cream

INGREDIENTS

4 1/2 lb/2kg mussels
3/4 cup/175mL dry white wine
1 tablespoon/15mL chopped parsley
a small bouquet garni (see Note)
1/3 cup/75mL butter
2 medium onions, finely chopped
1 clove garlic, chopped
3/4 cup/175mL hot milk
2 egg yolks
3/4 cup/175mL cream
3 tablespoons/45mL Pernod or lemon juice
freshly ground pepper
2 tablespoons/25mL chopped parsley
8 slices French bread
oil or butter for frying bread

METHOD

1. Clean the mussels and place in a large pan with the wine, parsley and bouquet garni. Cover and cook for about 5 minutes until the mussels are opened. Discard any unopened mussels. Strain the resulting broth through a fine sieve. Remove the top shell from the mussels and discard. Keep the mussels warm.

2. Heat the butter in a pan and sauté the onions and garlic gently until pale golden and soft. Add the strained mussel broth and 2 cups/500mL boiling water plus the milk. Simmer for 5 minutes.

3. Beat the egg yolks with the cream and Pernod or lemon juice. Stir in a little of the hot soup then return this mixture to the pa Reheat gently, stirring all the time. Season with pepper. Place the mussels in 4 large h soup plates, pour the hot sauce over and sprinkle with parsley.

4. Meanwhile, fry the bread in the oil or butter until golden on both sides. Serve wit the mussels.

Serves 4

Note: A bouquet garni is a bunch of herbs usually parsley, thyme, marjoram, rosemary a bay leaf, peppercorns and cloves–tied in muslin.

Clams in Green Sauce

INGREDIENTS

Green Sauce
2 tablespoons/25mL olive oil
2 tablespoons/25mL finely chopped onion
4 cloves garlic, minced
4 teaspoons/20mL all-purpose flour
1/4 cup/50mL dry white wine
1/4 cup/50mL plus 2 tablespoons/25mL fish broth or clam juice
2 tablespoons/25mL milk
1 small bunch parsley, finely chopped
salt and freshly ground pepper

1 dozen very small clams

METHOD

1. To make the green sauce, heat the oil in a frying pan and sauté the onion until it is wilted. Stir in the garlic. Add the flour and cook for 1 minute. Gradually pour in the wine, broth and milk and stir in the parsley, salt and pepper. Cook, stirring constantly, until thickened and smooth. May be prepared ahead.

2. Add the clams, cover and cook over low heat, removing the clams as they open. Return the clams to the sauce, making sure the clam meat is covered by the sauce. Ser from the pan.

Serves 1 .

MUSSELS IN PERNOD CREAM

Clams in White Wine Sauce

When clams (or mussels) are cooked and opened in a sauce, there is always the danger that they will release some sand. To minimize this possibility, place them for several hours or overnight in the refrigerator in a bowl of salted water sprinkled with one tablespoon/15mL of cornmeal. The clams will release any foreign materials and at the same time will become quite plump.

INGREDIENTS

7 tablespoons/105mL olive oil

2 tablespoons/25mL minced onion

4 cloves garlic, minced

2 dozen small clams, scrubbed, at room
   temperature

1 tablespoon/15mL all-purpose flour

1 tablespoon/15mL paprika

2 tablespoons/25mL minced parsley

1 cup/250mL semi-sweet white wine

1 bay leaf

1 dried red chili pepper, cut into 3 pieces,
   seeds removed

freshly ground pepper

salt

METHOD

1. Heat the oil in a large, shallow frying pan. Sauté the onion and garlic until the onion is wilted. Add the clams and cook, uncovered, over medium-high heat until they open. (If some open much sooner than others, remove them so they do not toughen. Return to the pan when all have opened.)

2. Sprinkle in the flour and stir, then add the paprika, parsley, wine, bay leaf, chili, pepper and salt, if necessary (the liquid the clams release may be salty). Continue cooking and stirring for another 5 minutes. Serve in the cooking dish if possible, and let everyone help themselves.

Serves 4–6

Stuffed Mussels

INGREDIENTS

18 medium-sized mussels
3/4 cup/175mL water
1 slice lemon
1 tablespoon/15mL olive oil
4 tablespoons/60mL minced onion
2 tablespoons/25mL minced cured ham
1 clove garlic, minced
1 teaspoon/5mL tomato sauce
1 tablespoon/15mL minced parsley
salt and freshly ground pepper

White Sauce

3 tablespoons/45mL butter
4 tablespoons/60mL all-purpose flour
1/2 cup/125mL milk
salt and freshly ground pepper

1 cup/250mL breadcrumbs
1 tablespoon/15mL grated cheese
2 eggs, lightly beaten with
   1 teaspoon/5mL water
oil, for frying

METHOD

1. Scrub the mussels well and remove the beards.

2. Place them in a pan with the water and lemon slice. Bring to the boil and remove the mussels as they open. Do not overcook. Reserve 1/2 cup/125mL of the mussel broth.

3. Mince the mussel meat. Separate the shells and discard half of them. Heat the olive oil in a small frying pan. Add the onion and sauté until it is wilted. Add the ham and garlic and sauté for 1 minute more. Stir in the tomato sauce, the minced mussel meat, parsley, salt and pepper. Cook for 5 minutes. Half-fill the mussel shells with this mixture.

4. To make the white sauce, melt the butter in a saucepan over moderate heat. Add the flour and stir for 2 minutes. Gradually pour in the reserved mussel broth and the milk. Cook, stirring constantly, until the sauce is smooth and thick. Season with salt and pepper. Remove the pan from the heat and cool slightly, stirring occasionally.

5. Using a teaspoon, cover the filled mussel shells with the white sauce, sealing the edges by smoothing with the cupped side of a spoon. Refrigerate for 1 hour or more, until the sauce hardens. (May be prepared ahead.)

6. Mix together the breadcrumbs and cheese. Dip the mussels into the beaten egg, then into the crumb mixture. Deep-fry the mussels filled-side down until they are well browned. Serve warm.

Serves 4–5

Sautéed Mussels

INGREDIENTS

18 medium-sized mussels
1/2 cup/125mL water
1 slice lemon
6 tablespoons/90mL olive oil
1 small onion, minced
1 clove garlic, minced
1 tablespoon/15mL minced parsley
1/2 teaspoon/2mL paprika, preferably
   Spanish style
1/2 dried and crumbled, or 1/4 teaspoon/1mL
   crushed, chili

METHOD

1. Place the mussels in a frying pan with the water and lemon slice. Bring to the boil and remove the mussels as they open. Do not overcook. Discard the shells and drain the mussel meat on paper towels.

2. Heat the oil in a medium-sized frying pan. Stir-fry the mussels for 1 minute and remove. Add the onion and garlic and sauté slowly, covered, for about 5 minutes. Remove from the heat. Stir in the parsley, paprika and chili. May be prepared ahead.

3. Return the frying pan to the heat and add the mussels (with their accumulated juices). Give the mussels a turn in the sauce just to heat them, remove from the heat, cover and set aside for 2 minutes before serving. The mussels may also be served at room temperature.

Serves 2

MUSSELS RIVIERA

Mussels Riviera

INGREDIENTS

Riviera Mix
olive oil
1 onion, finely chopped
2 garlic cloves, chopped
4 tomatoes, finely chopped
1/2 red bell pepper, chopped finely
1 cup/250mL white wine
**2 tablespoons/25mL rosemary, thyme
and basil mix, dry or freshly chopped**
salt, pepper and paprika

**2lb/1kg mussels, cooked mariniéres
style, in half shell (see page 48)**

**1 tablespoon/15mL grated
Parmesan cheese**

METHOD

1. Heat the oil, add the onion, garlic, tomatoes and bell pepper in a saucepan and cook slowly for 5 minutes.

2. Add white wine and herbs, season with salt, pepper and paprika. Cook slowly for 30 minutes until the mixture reaches a paste consistency.

3. Using a spoon, cover the mussels with the paste, top with Parmesan. Place under the grill and heat until the Parmesan has lightly browned. Serve with focaccia bread.

Serves 4

Lemon and Garlic Steamed Mussels

INGREDIENTS

**2 dozen small or
medium-sized mussels**
3 tablespoons/45mL olive oil
**2 tablespoons/25mL fresh
lemon juice**
2 cloves garlic, minced

METHOD

1. Place the mussels in a frying pan without water. Cover and cook over medium heat, removing the mussels to a warm platter as they open. Discard any that do not open.

2. Reduce the liquid in the frying pan to about 2–3 tablespoons/25–45mL, then return the mussels to the pan. Sprinkle with the oil, lemon juice and garlic and heat for 1 minute. Serve immediately, with plenty of good bread for dunking.

Serves 2

Clams Waterzooi

INGREDIENTS

1 tablespoon/15mL olive oil
2lb/1kg clams, cleaned
1¹/₂ cups/375mL dry white wine
5 cups/1.25L chicken or fish stock
8oz/225g Yukon Gold potatoes, peeled
    and cut in large dices (2 small)
1 cup/250mL carrots, peeled and
    sliced finely
1 cup/250mL leeks (white part only),
    sliced and washed
1 cup/250mL celery, sliced and washed
1 tablespoon/15mL cornstarch mixed with
    2 tablespoons/25mL water
¹/₃ cup/75mL Devon or whipping cream
salt and pepper
1 tablespoon/15mL chopped parsley

METHOD

1. Place the oil, clams and white wine in a large pot over high heat. Cook until all have opened.

2. Remove the clams and set aside.

3. Put the remaining broth and stock together in pot, bring to the boil, add the potatoes and cook for 10 minutes.

4. Add the carrots, leeks and celery and cook until the potatoes are cooked (around 8–10 minutes).

5. Strain the cooking liquid out of the vegetables and pour it into a large pot (on high heat). Keep the vegetables and potatoes aside.

6. Bring the pot to the boil, add the cornstarch mixture and boil until thickened (around 1 minute). Add the cream, salt and pepper to taste and boil for another 30 seconds.

7. Add the clams and vegetables, bring back to the boil and serve in a large soup bowl or in individual plates. Garnish with parsley. Serve with dry white wine.

Serves 4

Baked Clams

INGREDIENTS

1 dozen clams, cooked mariniéres style
  (see page 48)
4 tablespoons/60mL butter
2 large cloves garlic, minced
2 tablespoons/25mL minced onion
2 tablespoons/25mL minced parsley
¹/₄ teaspoon/1mL paprika
¹/₄ teaspoon/1mL thyme
salt and freshly ground pepper
3 teaspoons/15mL breadcrumbs
¹/₄ teaspoon/1mL olive oil

METHOD

1. Remove one shell from each clam and loosen the meat from the remaining shell. Melt the butter in a frying pan and sauté the garlic, onion, parsley, paprika, thyme, salt and pepper for 2 minutes, stirring. Cover the clams with this mixture.

2. Mix the breadcrumbs with the oil. Sprinkle over the clams. (May be prepared ahead.) Heat under the grill until browned.

Makes 12

CLAMS WATERZOOI

Mussel Risotto

INGREDIENTS

7/8 cup/200mL olive oil

1 onion, finely chopped

2 cloves garlic, finely chopped

1 red bell pepper, diced

1¼ cups/300mL arborio rice

2¼ cups/550mL dry white wine

2lb/1kg mussels, cleaned

1 tablespoon/15mL chopped fresh
   aromatic herbs (thyme,
   rosemary, marjoram)

2 tablespoons/25mL grated
   Parmesan cheese

METHOD

1. Place the oil in a pot over medium heat.

2. Add the onion, garlic and bell pepper and cook for 2 minutes.

3. Add rice and half the wine. Stir with a wooden spatula and cook until the rice is almost dry.

4. Add the mussels and the other half of the wine.

5. Add the herbs and cook until the rice and mussels are cooked. Replace the lid and stir frequently to avoid the rice sticking to the pot.

6. Serve sprinkled with grated Parmesan.

Serves 4

MUSSELS WITH
LIME MAYONNAISE

Mussels with Lime Mayonnaise

INGREDIENTS
3lb/1¹⁄₂kg mussels

1 egg

2 teaspoons/10mL each of vinegar and
    lime juice

¹⁄₂ teaspoon/2mL salt

1 teaspoon/5mL French mustard

1¹⁄₄ cups/300mL light olive oil

carrot, for garnishing

¹⁄₄ bunch fresh cilantro or chives

METHOD

1. Scrub the mussels and steam them open. Remove the top shells and cut the mussels from the bottom shells, leaving them in place. Set aside, covered, in the refrigerator.

2. Place the egg, vinegar, lime juice, salt and mustard in the bowl of a food processor and process for about 20 seconds. While the machine is running, add the oil in a thin, steady stream. It is important to keep the consistency of the mayonnaise thick, so stop every now and then to check. Taste for seasoning, adding some pepper if desired. The result should be a thick emulsion. To thin, add 1 or 2 spoonfuls of hot water, beating well.

3. Meanwhile, peel the carrot and cut into long thin strips. Arrange the carrot strips on 6 plates and top with the mussels in their half shells.

4. Spoon a little lime mayonnaise on each and garnish each mussel with a little chopped cilantro or chives.

Serves 3–4

Mussels in Garlic Butter

INGREDIENTS
¹⁄₂ cup/125mL butter or margarine, cubed

2 cloves garlic, crushed

4 tablespoons/60mL chopped parsley

2 dozen mussels, washed, beards
    removed

¹⁄₄ cup/50mL chopped shallots

2 sprigs thyme

1 bay leaf

pinch salt

1 cup/250mL dry white wine

METHOD

1. Cream the butter in a bowl with the garlic and parsley.

2. Place the mussels in a saucepan with the remaining ingredients. Bring to the boil and simmer for 3 minutes or until the mussels open. Detach the lid of the mussels from the base and place the mussels, still sitting in the shell, on a baking sheet.

3. Dot generously with the garlic butter and grill until the butter has melted.

Serves 2

Pernod Baked Mussels

INGREDIENTS

1/4 cup/50mL mussel cooking
   broth, strained
1 onion, chopped
1 clove garlic, chopped
1/4 cup/50mL white wine
1/3 cup/75mL Devon or whipping cream
2 tablespoons/25mL Pernod
juice of 1/2 lemon
salt and pepper
2lb/1kg mussels cleaned, cooked
   mariniéres style (see page 48)
   and divided in half shells

METHOD

1. Place the broth, onion, garlic and white wine in a pot and cook over high heat, until reduced to a quarter.

2. Add the cream and reduce again to half.

3. Add the Pernod, lemon juice, salt and pepper.

4. Cover the mussels with the sauce.

5. Heat under the grill for 2 minutes and serve.

Serves 4

Saffron Rice with Seafood

INGREDIENTS
good pinch of Spanish saffron
3 cups/750mL fish or chicken stock
2 tablespoons/25mL olive oil
2 onions, chopped
1¼ cups/300mL long-grain rice, rinsed
8oz/250g green prawns (shrimp), shelled
    and deveined
8oz/250g scallops
12 mussels or baby clams, cleaned
small bunch cilantro

METHOD
1. Heat the saffron in the stock and leave to
infuse. Heat the olive oil in frying pan, paella or
flattish casserole dish and gently cook the
onions until soft and golden. Add the rice and
cook, stirring until well coated with oil. Add the
hot stock, stirring until mixture comes to the
boil, reduce the heat and simmer gently for
10 minutes.

2. Add the prawns (shrimp) and scallops,
pressing gently into the rice. Continue to cook
for 5 minutes. Add the prepared mussels or
clams, which should open with the heat. If you
have a lid, partly cover the rice. When the rice
is tender (about 18–20 minutes) remove from
the heat and gently fork it up. Sprinkle cilantro
sprigs over and serve.

Serves 6

Potato Gnocchi and Pesto Mussels

INGREDIENTS

Pesto

1 handful of basil leaves

1 handful of flat-leaf (Italian) parsley leaves

2/3 cup/150mL virgin olive oil

1/2 cup/125mL grated Parmesan

6 cloves garlic, crushed

salt and pepper

1 tablespoon/15mL pine nuts

10oz/285g potato and semolina gnocchi (or other type)

1/4 cup/50mL olive oil

1 onion, finely chopped

1lb/500g black mussels, cleaned

1/2 cup/125mL dry white wine

3 vine-ripened tomatoes, diced

1/2 cup/125mL grated Parmesan cheese

METHOD

1. To prepare the pesto, blend all the ingredients together until you reach a smooth paste consistency.

2. Cook the gnocchi in boiling water for around 5 minutes.

3. While gnocchi are cooking, place the oil in a large pot on medium heat and add the onion. Cook for 1 minute.

4. Add the mussels, white wine and tomatoes and cook with the lid on.

5. When the mussels are cooked (about 5 minutes), add the gnocchi and pesto. Mix well.

6. Serve hot with grated Parmesan.

Serves 3–4

Saffron and Clam Risotto

INGREDIENTS

½ cup/125mL virgin olive oil

1 onion, finely sliced

4 cloves garlic, finely chopped

2 cups/500mL arborio rice

1½ cups/375mL dry white wine

pinch of saffron (powder or thread)

2 cups/500mL chicken stock

salt and pepper

1 tablespoon/15mL mixed fresh herbs, chopped

2lb/1kg surf clams

METHOD

1. On medium heat put the virgin olive oil, onion and garlic in a large pot and cook for 1 minute with a lid.

2. Add the rice and stir with a wooden spatula.

3. Add the white wine and saffron and cook slowly until the rice starts becoming dry (around 5 minutes).

4. Add the chicken stock, seasoning, mixed herbs and surf clams and cook until all the shells have opened and the rice is cooked (around 15 minutes). Keep stirring frequently to avoid the rice sticking to the pot.

5. Serve with salad and/or crispy ciabatta bread.

Serves 4

Spinach Mornay Mussels

INGREDIENTS

2lb/1kg mussels, cleaned
2 tablespoons/25mL butter
3 tablespoons/45mL all-purpose flour
1³/4 cups/425mL milk
salt, pepper and nutmeg
1³/4 cups/425mL grated Cheddar
1/2 cup/125mL grated Parmesan cheese
5oz/150g spinach, blanched and chopped

METHOD

1. Cook the mussels mariniéres style
(see page 48) and remove 1 shell from
each mussel.

2. Melt the butter slowly in a pot. Do not allow
the butter to burn.

3. Add the flour and mix until very smooth, using
a wooden spatula. Remove from the heat.

4. Add the milk with a whisk and return to the
heat. Stir with the whisk until boiling. Reduce the
heat and cook slowly for 5 minutes. Season with
salt, pepper and nutmeg.

5. Add the cheeses. Cook for another 5 minutes
on low heat, until the cheese is completely
melted.

6. Top up the half-shell mussels with the mornay
sauce and spinach and heat under the grill until
golden brown.

Serves 3–4

Smoked Salmon and Asparagus Mussels

INGREDIENTS

200mL/7fl oz Mousseline Sauce
   (see page 86)
2lb/1kg black mussels, cooked and
   separated in half shells
2 bunches asparagus, poached in water
   and cut into small ¹/₂in/1cm long sticks
5oz/150g sliced smoked salmon, shredded
   with a sharp knife

METHOD

1. Prepare Mousseline Sauce.

2. Remove the mussels from the shell and top each shell with asparagus.

3. Place the mussels back in the shells and sprinkle with the shredded smoked salmon.

4. Top each mussel with Mousseline Sauce.

5. Place under the grill for 5 minutes or until the mousseline has a golden brown color.

Serves 3–4

EXOTIC FLAVORS

Blue Cheese Mussels

INGREDIENTS

2 tablespoons/25mL olive oil
1 onion, chopped
1 stalk celery, sliced
1/2 leek, sliced
2lb/1kg mussels, cleaned
1/2 cup/125mL white wine
2oz/50g blue cheese, broken into
   small pieces
1 handful of fresh spinach leaves
juice of 1 lemon
2 tablespoons/25mL butter
1 tablespoon/15mL chopped parsley

METHOD

1. Place the oil, onion, celery and leek in a pot and cook for 2 minutes, stirring frequently.

2. Add the mussels, white wine, blue cheese, spinach, lemon juice and cook until the mussels have opened.

3. Add the butter and parsley, stir and serve.

Serves 3–4

Pacific Rim Mussels

INGREDIENTS

2 tablespoons/25mL vegetable oil
1 small onion, finely chopped
2 cloves garlic, crushed
1 teaspoon/5mL grated fresh ginger
1 teaspoon/5mL hot curry paste
1 teaspoon/5mL ground allspice
pinch cayenne pepper
14oz/398mL can chopped tomatoes
2 lime leaves, shredded
salt and pepper
1 1/2lb/750mL large fresh mussels,
   scrubbed and cleaned, beards
   removed
1 tablespoon/15mL chopped fresh
   cilantro, to garnish

METHOD

1. Heat the oil in the bottom of a double boiler or large saucepan. Add the onion, garlic, ginger, curry paste and spices and fry gently for 10 minutes until softened.

2. Add the chopped tomatoes and shredded lime leaves, cover and simmer for 20 minutes until thickened. Season to taste with salt and pepper.

3. Place the mussels either in the top of the double boiler, or in a steamer set over the saucepan. Steam the mussels over the sauce for 5 minutes. Discard any mussels which do not open.

4. Carefully discard one half of each mussel shell and arrange the mussels in individual serving dishes. Spoon the sauce over and serve at once garnished with the chopped cilantro.

Serves 6

LUE CHEESE MUSSELS

Chinese-Style Mussels

INGREDIENTS

Sauce

1/2 cup/125mL oyster sauce

1 tablespoon/15mL fresh chopped ginger

1 red chili, sliced

1 clove garlic, chopped

1 tablespoon/15mL white vinegar

1 tablespoon/15mL soy sauce

pinch Chinese 5 spices

1 tablespoon/15mL sesame oil

2lb/1kg mussels cleaned

1/4 cup/50mL water

1 tablespoon/15mL cornstarch or
   arrowroot mixed with
   2 tablespoons/25mL cold water

1 tablespoon/15mL cilantro, chopped

3 shallots, finely chopped

rice or noodles to serve

METHOD

1. Mix all the sauce ingredients together.

2. Place the sesame oil, mussels and water in a pot and cook until the mussels start to open.

3. Add the sauce and cook until all the mussels are open.

4. Add the cornstarch (or arrowroot) mixture and stir until the sauce thickens. This should take around 1 minute.

5. Add the cilantro and shallots. Serve with rice or noodles.

Serves 4

Curry Mussels

INGREDIENTS

2 tablespoons/25mL olive oil
1 small onion, chopped
1 stalk celery, sliced
1 clove garlic, chopped
2 tablespoons/25mL yellow curry paste
2 cardamom pods, crushed
pinch ground cumin
2lb/1kg mussels, cleaned
¼ cup/50mL coconut cream
1 tablespoon/15mL fresh chopped cilantro
chopped chili (optional)

METHOD

1. Place the oil, onion, celery, garlic, curry paste, cardamom and cumin in a pot and cook on slow heat for 5 minutes, stirring frequently.

2. Add the mussels and coconut cream and cook over high heat.

3. Cook until all the mussels have opened, stirring every minute to ensure the mussels are cooked evenly.

4. Add the cilantro, stir and serve. Add chopped chili if you like it very spicy.

Serves 2

Goan Curry with Clams and Raita

INGREDIENTS

Raita

1/2 cucumber, peeled, center removed,
  diced
1 tablespoon/15mL chopped fresh mint
5 tablespoons/75mL plain yogurt
juice of 1 lemon
salt and pepper, to taste

Curry

2 tablespoons/25mL oil
1 onion, sliced finely
2 cloves garlic, chopped
1 tablespoon/15mL cumin powder
1 tablespoon/15mL turmeric powder
2 tablespoons/25mL mild curry powder
1 tablespoon/15mL ginger powder
2 cardamom pods, cracked
pinch chili powder
1/4 stick cinnamon, cracked
2lb/1kg clams, cleaned and free of sand
3 tablespoons/45mL water
1/4 cup/50mL coconut cream
1 tablespoon/15mL fresh chopped
  cilantro leaves
2 tablespoons/25mL oil
basmati rice or curried vegetables to serve

METHOD

1. Combine the raita ingredients and set aside.

2. Over medium heat in a large cooking pot, add the oil, onion, garlic and all the spices. Cook for 2 minutes, gently.

3. Add the clams and water. Cook until all the clams have opened. Stir frequently.

4. When the clams are opening, add the coconut cream and cilantro.

5. Serve in a large bowl with basmati rice or curried vegetables, with the raita mix on the side.

Mussels in Ginger with Pesto Crumb Topping

INGREDIENTS

4¹/₂lb/2kg mussels

¹/₂ cup/125mL dry white wine

2 cloves garlic, crushed

4 slices Parma ham (prosciutto),
   finely chopped

1¹/₂ cups/375mL fresh white breadcrumbs

2 tablespoons/25mL pesto

2 tablespoons/25mL grated fresh ginger

METHOD

1. Scrub the mussels. Soak them in cold water for 5 minutes, drain, then repeat. Remove any beards and discard any mussels that are open or damaged. Place in a large saucepan with the wine and garlic. Cover and cook over high heat for 3 minutes or until the mussels open, shaking the pan occasionally. Discard any mussels that do not open.

2. Remove the mussels from the pan and reserve the cooking liquid. Discard the top shell from each mussel and arrange the mussels on the half shell on a baking sheet. Strain the mussel liquid through muslin or a clean kitchen cloth. Combine the ham, breadcrumbs, pesto and ginger and stir in 1–2 spoonfuls of the mussel liquid to moisten.

3. Preheat the grill to high. Spoon a little crumb mixture onto each mussel, then cook under the grill for 2 minutes or until golden and bubbling.

Serves 4

Laksa

INGREDIENTS

3 tablespoons/45mL peanut or
  vegetable oil
1 onion, finely chopped
3 cloves garlic, chopped
1 tablespoon/15mL laksa paste (spicy
  shrimp paste)
1³/4 cups/125mL chicken stock
1 stick lemon grass, chopped
1lb/500g mussels, cleaned
8fl oz/250mL coconut cream
5oz/150g rice noodles
1 lime leaf, finely chopped

METHOD

1. Place the oil, onion, garlic and laksa paste in
a large cooking pot and cook for 3–5 minutes
over medium heat.

2. Add the chicken stock and lemon grass.
Add mussels and cook until the mussels
start to open.

3. Add the coconut cream, rice noodles and
lime leaf. Cook for a further 4 minutes.

4. Serve when all the mussels have opened.

Serves 4

Mussels Parquee

INGREDIENTS

24 large black mussels
1 red Spanish onion, chopped very finely
1 red chili, chopped very finely
1/3 cup/75mL aged red wine vinegar
1/4 cup/50mL red port wine
salt and pepper, to taste
lemon wedges, to serve

METHOD

1. Open the mussels raw, using a small knife.

2. Combine all the other ingredients, except the lemon wedges, together and set aside.

3. Place the mussels on a serving plate and top with the mixture.

4. Refrigerate for 5 minutes and serve with lemon wedges.

Serves 2

MUSSELS PARQUEE

Mussels Tin Tin

INGREDIENTS

1/4 cup/50mL white wine
1 red chili, sliced
1 stalk lemon grass, crushed
1 tablespoon/15mL fresh chopped ginger
1 clove garlic, chopped
1 tablespoon/15mL peanut oil
2lb/1kg mussels, cleaned
1/2 cup/125mL coconut cream
1 tablespoon/15mL fresh cilantro, chopped

METHOD

1. Place the white wine, chili, lemon grass, ginger and garlic in a pot and infuse together for 15 minutes.

2. In a separate pot, gently heat the oil and mussels. Add to the ingredients above.

3. Add the coconut cream and cook until the mussels have opened, stirring frequently.

4. Stir in the cilantro and serve.

Serves 2

EXOTIC FLAVORS

Spanish Marinated Mussels

INGREDIENTS

2lb/1kg mussels, cooked mariniéres
  style (see page 48) and taken out of the
  shell
1 hard-boiled egg (white only),
  chopped finely
2 tablespoons/25mL baby capers
2 tablespoons/25mL fresh aromatic herbs
  (thyme, rosemary, marjoram), chopped

2 vine-ripened tomatoes, finely chopped
2/3 cup/150mL Spanish virgin olive oil
1 tablespoon/15mL Dijon mustard
2 tablespoons/25mL old sherry vinegar
1 tablespoon/15mL fresh basil,
  roughly chopped
salt and pepper

METHOD

1. Combine all the ingredients and marinate in the refrigerator for 2 hours.

2. Serve with salad or as tapas with a glass of wine.

Serves 4

Clams in Black Beans

INGREDIENTS

Black Bean Sauce
4 tablespoons/60mL fermented black beans
  (also called salted black beans)
1 tablespoon/15mL fresh chopped ginger
1 chopped red chili
2 garlic cloves, chopped
1 tablespoon/15mL white vinegar
2 tablespoons/25mL soy sauce
pinch Chinese 5 spices
1 teaspoon/5mL sugar
2 tablespoons/25mL vegetable oil

1 tablespoon/15mL sesame oil
2lb/1 kg clams, cleaned and sand removed
1/4 cup/50mL water
1/2 cup/155mL black bean sauce
1 tablespoon/15mL cornstarch, mixed
  with 2 tablespoons/25mL water
1 tablespoon/15mL cilantro, chopped
3 green onions, finely chopped
rice or noodles to serve

METHOD

1. Rinse the fermented black beans thoroughly and then mince (not rinsing the beans will make the sauce too salty). Mix all the sauce ingredients, set aside for 15 minutes.

2. On high heat and in a large pot, put the sesame oil, clams and water and cook until the clams start to open.

3. Add the sauce mix and cook until all the clams have opened.

4. Add the cornstarch and stir until the sauce has thickened, around 1 minute on high heat.

5. Add the cilantro and green onions.

6. Serve with rice or noodles.

Serves 4

CLAMS IN BLACK BEANS

Mussels in Coconut Vinegar

INGREDIENTS

3lb/1¹/₂kg mussels in their shells

6 whole cilantro sprigs, washed
and roughly chopped

3 stalks fresh lemon grass, chopped,
or 1¹/₂ teaspoons/7mL dried lemon grass,
soaked in hot water until soft

2in/5cm piece fresh ginger, shredded

¹/₂ cup/125mL water

1 tablespoon/15mL vegetable oil

1 red onion, halved and sliced

2 fresh red chilies, sliced

2 tablespoons/25mL coconut vinegar

fresh cilantro, chopped

METHOD

1. Place mussels, cilantro, lemon grass, ginger and water in a wok over a high heat. Cover and cook for 5 minutes or until the mussels open. Discard any mussels that do not open after 5 minutes of cooking. Remove the mussels from the wok, discard the cilantro, lemon grass and ginger. Strain the cooking liquid and reserve.

2. Heat the oil in a wok over a medium heat, add the onion and chilies and stir-fry for 3 minutes or until the onion is soft. Add the mussels, reserved cooking liquid and coconut vinegar and stir-fry for 2 minutes or until the mussels are heated. Scatter with cilantro and serve.

Serves 4

Shellfish in Lemon Grass

INGREDIENTS

5 red or golden shallots, chopped
4 stalks fresh lemon grass, cut into
   1¹/₄in/3cm pieces, or
   2 teaspoons/10mL dried lemon grass,
   soaked in hot water until soft
3 cloves garlic, chopped
2in/5cm piece fresh ginger, grated
3 fresh red chilies, seeded and chopped
8 kaffir lime leaves, torn into pieces
1¹/₂lb/750g mussels, scrubbed
   and beards removed
¹/₄ cup/50mL water
12 scallops on shells, cleaned
1 tablespoon/15mL lime juice
1 tablespoon/15mL Thai fish sauce
   (nam pla)
3 tablespoons/45mL fresh basil leaves

METHOD

1. Place the shallots, lemon grass, garlic, ginger, chilies and lime leaves in a small bowl and mix to combine.

2. Place the mussels in a wok and sprinkle over half the shallot mixture. Pour in the water, cover and cook over a high heat for 5 minutes.

3. Add the scallops, remaining shallot mixture, lime juice, fish sauce (nam pla) and basil and toss to combine. Cover and cook for 4–5 minutes or until the mussels and scallops are cooked. Discard any mussels that do not open after 5 minutes.

Serves 4

INDEX

INDEX

FAVORITES

FAVORITES

FAVORITES